Chris O'mone

The SAGA
of the
Early WARRI Princes

A History of the Beginnings of a
West African Dynasty

1480–1654

iUniverse, Inc.
Bloomington

The Saga of the Early Warri Princes
A History of the Beginnings of a West African Dynasty, 1480–1654

iUniverse books may be ordered through booksellers or by contacting:

iUniverse
1663 Liberty Drive
Bloomington, IN 47403
www.iuniverse.com
1-800-Authors (1-800-288-4677)

Because of the dynamic nature of the Internet, any web addresses or links contained in this book may have changed since publication and may no longer be valid. The views expressed in this work are solely those of the author and do not necessarily reflect the views of the publisher, and the publisher hereby disclaims any responsibility for them.

Any people depicted in stock imagery provided by Thinkstock are models, and such images are being used for illustrative purposes only.

Certain stock imagery © Thinkstock.

ISBN: 978-1-4620-8427-2 (sc)
ISBN: 978-1-4620-8429-6 (e)
ISBN: 978-1-4620-8428-9 (dj)

Library of Congress Control Number: 2011963115

Printed in the United States of America

iUniverse rev. date: 1/16/2012

Contents

West Africa

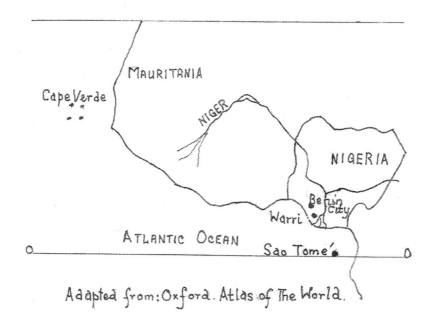

Adapted from: Oxford. Atlas of The World.

Preface

This story chronicles Prince Iginua's exile from the Edo Kingdom in West Africa during the late fifteenth century. On his journey south, he was accompanied by a loyal Court whose support remained unchanged even after his death. His early descendants survived the perils of a new and strange environment as the early Princes of a West African Dynasty, the Iginua/Ginuwa Dynasty, into the sixteenth and seventeenth centuries.

At times, this account differs from and expands on accepted or customary Edo and Itsekiri lore. However, as the lives of Dom Domingos and his son, António Domingos, suggest, a treasure of historical knowledge and information awaits research and opinions about Ueri and its relations with Edo Kingdom and Portugal in the fifteenth, sixteenth, and seventeenth centuries.

I could not have written this book without sources that include, but are not limited to the institutions and the authors of the texts that I have acknowledged and to whom I am indebted.

I wish to thank friends who encouraged and helped me during the preparation of this manuscript, including Lisa Haywood, Zoe McNair, Roberta Parris-Toney, and Sister Esimi Gbubemi Affoh. I'm grateful to my nephew, Dr. Paul (Pablo) Idahosa, Professor of African and Development Studies at York University, Canada, for undertaking the unenviable task of advisor and facilitator; but I take responsibility for all errors or incorrect inclusions in the work.

C. O.

The Ginuwa Dynasty

Dates of the Enthronement of the Warri Princes

Early: Pre-Christian
ca. 1480 Iginua (Ginuwa) Odihi n'ame
ca. 1500 Ijijen (Ogbowuru) The Unheralded Prince
ca. 1525 Irame
ca. 1550 Ojoluwa
ca. 1570 Esigie

Christian
1597 Sebastian aka Eyomasan; Aronrongboye
1625 Dom Domingos
1643 António Domingos, aka Oyenakpagha;
Omonigheren (Prince with the Golden Skin)

Later Christian
1654 Matthias Ludivico (aka Omoluyiri)
1674 Luigi (aka Abejoye)
1701 Sebastian II (aka Akenjoye)
1709 Miguel (aka Omagboye)
ca. 1710 Dom Agostinho (aka Akengboye)
ca. 1735 Atogbuwa (Non-Christian)
1760 Manuel Otobia (aka Erejuwa)
1807 Joao (aka Akengbua)

Chris O'mone

1848–1936 Interregnum

ca. = about ± 5–10 years

Adapted from: J.O.S. Ayomike, 1993 and *Sunday Tribune* (Nigeria), March 1, 1987.

Edo Origins: Iginua, Exile from Edo Kingdom and First Warri Prince

This story is a narrative of a Prince, the loyalists that accompanied him into exile and descendants who joined the people of a marginal Itsekiri land to create a kingdom and establish a West African dynasty. Our saga begins, if it could be said to have had only one beginning, in the ancient Kingdom of Benin or the Edo Kingdom as the purist might choose to call it. The Edo Kingdom lies inland from the eastern portion of a bay in the mid-Atlantic Ocean known as the Bight of Benin, which washes over the West Coast of Africa. The kingdom never extended to the Atlantic shoreline because the costal predominantly mangrove marshlands of the riverines and the Niger Delta separate its southern rain forest environs from the sea. It reaches inland in a north to north easterly direction of modern day southwestern Nigeria to a section of the western bank of the lordly river Niger and contiguous Kurkuruku Mountains. The flat, forest landscape of the south changes gradually through beautiful, thinly forested hills and valleys in the midlands to the scrublands of the hills to the far north and east. In such diverse terrain, farmers, hunters, lumbermen, and a few fishermen flourished. Commerce developed to market their products and created a middle class that in turn demanded sophisticated artisan goods made from wood, iron, bronze, and terra cotta.

The organized multistratal society that evolved became the

Edo Kingdom. It founded a civilization with its center in Ubini, a city that became known to the external world as Benin City. Seven centuries after the city was first described by early Portuguese explorers, the city remains famous for traces of its original wall and moat, its street grids, and Palace Square.

The title of the leader of this structured society remains Omo n' Oba' n' Edo uku Akpolokpolo. In peace, the leader headed a Court that maintained the law and order that secured the stability and the kingdom's vibrant economy. In war, the "Oba", as in the title *Omo n'Oba n'Edo*, led the Edo Army into battle to defend the integrity of the kingdom.

Iginua: Exile and First Warri Prince

In approximately 1473, Oba Olua succeeded to the title and its responsibilities. He ruled for eight years. In the preceding decade, the kingdom's commerce had acquired a new dimension. Portuguese explorers reached Benin City, whose existence had been rumored in Europe for more than a century. The explorers navigated the riverines with the help of the Itsekiris, whose early ancestors are thought to have arrived in successive waves from the Ijebu hinterland. Peppers, bronze objects, leopard skins, and elephant tusks were exchanged with the Portuguese for silk, coral beads, and other personal items that initially became popular among the elite and then the general populace. Between 1475 and 1480, direct trade between the parties suffered a setback, and the Portuguese traders were satisfied to drop anchor in the riverines and designate the Itsekiris as their middlemen. It was not long before the consequences of the Portuguese traders' withdrawal reverberated throughout the city and beyond. While the increase in prices of the foreign items imposed by the Itsekiris was an outrage to those from all sections of the society, the families of Court Officers also could cite a personal impact of declining purchasing power resulting from a shortfall at the Treasury.

During this period of public and social discontent, a Prince was coming of age. Intelligent but unpretentious, Iginua had distinguished himself as an affably mannered scholar whose good nature made him popular among his peers, siblings, and supervisors at the Palace School. He had become a city-smart Prince. His personal attributes had apparently transformed a small circle of Court friends and admirers into an overt and sizeable following inside and outside the palace. The Oba and his Court were preoccupied with pressing matters of State that were compounded by the inflationary pressures on the economy, which were precipitated by the trading activities of the otherwise friendly Itsekiri neighbors. The unexpected increasing popularity of a charismatic junior Prince of a Dynasty, without a primogeniture tradition of succession was of grave concern. Legend held that succession struggles were divisive; their aftermaths were characterized by enduring rancor. Not many in the hierarchy wanted to witness one such event during their watch.

The commemorative ancestral rites of 1478 were exceptional. The crowds were thrilled by the performances of the dancers and drummers; the sacrificial ceremonies were clean and classic; the festive boards sagged under mounds of food. But before the acclaim abated and the good will generated by the offerings forfeited, the Oba and his Court acted.

The adolescent Prince Iginua was summoned to an audience, before which the strategy for resolving the kingdom's economic crisis was outlined. The riverine settlements would become a subordinate kingdom, and Iginua had been nominated as its ruler with the title of Prince of the Rivers, "Odihi N'ame." Some members of the Edo Court had accepted the privilege of accompanying and helping Iginua to establish a Court in the Edo tradition. A limited number of friends and confidants in the city were allowed to join his entourage. The Prince's primary duty was to control and supervise the Portuguese trade in the riverines. He would levy and collect taxes on the foreign goods. Half of the revenue was to be transmitted to the Edo Treasury at each harvest to compensate, in part, the families whose members were "volunteers" in his retinue.

In his proclamation, the Oba announced he was confident that the young and energetic Prince would accept the challenge of an assignment designed to enhance the long-term stability of the kingdom. The safe completion of the project was entrusted to Olokun, the Sea God, who had been generously appeased at the successful ancestral rites. Members of the Court who had given their support to the Oba commended the altruism demonstrated in the decision to send the Prince into service of the nation and end the Court's involvement and responsibilities in the Portuguese trade. Others loyal to the Prince maintained that his exile, and in effect theirs, had been masterfully disguised as an appeal for service and sacrifice for the sole purpose of removing a popular and potentially viable succession candidate.

The Prince had no choice; the Oba had spoken. Palace traditions expected unqualified obedience to the Oba's commands. He and his loyalists could now concentrate on the preparations necessary for launching their mission—one that fortuitously enabled the emergence of a new Dynasty and this Saga of the Early Warri Princes.

There was a sense of purpose, even urgency, at the various worksites where teams of artisans fashioned and assembled gear. Volunteers sorted and arranged donated or acquired material and supplies, ready for transportation. The eagerness and dedication was attributed in some measure to Prince Iginua's personal involvement in the supervision and coordination of the components of the preparatory activities. This was a contrast to a retreat of sulking or brooding in the isolation and safety of the Palace which would have been legitimate. It was also an inspiration that boosted the morale of his supporters. They had now become totally committed in their loyalty and enthusiasm; they completed all of their assignments by the projected time of departure from the river port of Ughoton early in the rainy season of 1479.

The preceding dry season had facilitated outdoor construction work without significant interruptions from rain. The consequent early accomplishment of the volunteers' tasks coincided with a favorable time for departure. The early rainy season assured a high water level sufficient to provide favorable floating conditions of the loaded watercraft, wooden trunks, and other containers in the flotilla. The downstream swiftness would enable early arrival of the mission at its destination camp and therefore avoid the predictable muddy ground working conditions of the late rainy season.

These were the circumstances at the departure of Prince Iginua and his volunteer" retinue of young and old, courtiers and priests, journeymen and volunteer guards when they bade their obligatory farewell at the Palace and embarked on their voyage to a de facto exile in Itsekiriland.

Loyalty and Success;
Survival and Severance

For centuries, the Itsekiris occupied their homeland settlements on the banks of the Benin, Escravos, and the Warri Rivers and their tributaries or on various islands located in the riverines. Because the language of the Itsekiris contains numerous words or their modifications in the modern Yoruba-Ijebu language, a linguistic marker has been advanced as the most viable indicator of their origin as is illustrated by the following basic time frame table:

English	Yesterday	Today	Tomorrow
Yoruba-Ijebu	Ola	Oni	Ojumo
Itsekiri	Ola	Onuwe	Ejuma

According to this thesis, the majority of early Itsekiris arrived as successive new waves of immigrants from Ijebuland. Aside from an undeniable accommodating and friendly nature that speaks to their immigrant origins, the uniformity and absence of dialects in the Itsekiri language, despite the apparent isolation of settlements, favors a single origin concept.

This latter characteristic also reflects the freedom of movement among the changing or generational populations that was encouraged by a uniform taboo of marriages among members of individual settlements, who probably emigrated as a group of family members. The favored intersettlement marriages required unrestricted movement and relations. It also encouraged a sharing of values, customs, and language. Eventually, and without conflict, it fostered the creation of one people with a common heritage in a loose federation of autonomous settlements.

A taboo is, in essence, an unwritten law. Compliance with the proscription of marriage between natives of individual settlements through successive generations implies a law-abiding way of life. Indeed, order and discipline in the settlements were overseen rather than enforced by the Olori Aja (settlement head) and his circle of Elders. The legitimacy of the Elders was based on the community's deference to age. That deference was coupled with a charge to accept responsibility for ensuring continuity.

One settlement of this predominantly aquatic environment of isolated small communities had been chosen as the Prince's destination. Ijala interrupted its routine briefly to welcome Prince Iginua and his entourage as a special wave of immigrants from the Edo Kingdom. The settlement then returned to its usual way of life while their Elders negotiated details of the immigrants' stay. Only a relatively small, in Edo terms, viable piece of land was available for assignment to the new immigrants. It was obvious some adaptation needed to be made in the lifestyle by the new settlers. The residents paid no special homage to the Prince, and certainly no acclamation. No landmass was available to be appropriated nor a populace to be governed in this supposed subordinate kingdom of the Oba's proclamation to which Iginua had been exiled or, more accurately, expelled.

With time on his hands, as the camp took form, Prince Iginua contemplated his past, his present, and his future. In the changed circumstances of his life, it seemed that his survival depended on the preservation of the sense of kinship, unity of purpose, and, above all, the loyalty that had emerged in his supporters since they were brought together by fate or forces beyond their control. To his way of thinking, it would be prudent to conduct the forthcoming trade operations with the Portuguese in a manner that would bring significant benefit to his supporters. And, in that manner, he would demonstrate that their partnership, rather than their participation, was essential for their survival and success of the mission. On a personal note, the Prince knew that sometime in the future,—a very distant future perhaps— he would seek a consort and begin a new family.

Achieving these goals, however, required action in the present. This included adopting the Edo Court Calendar and its related observances or rites that celebrated their common heritage. Work timetables, and descriptions defined individual responsibilities and contributions to the advancement of the community. They also combated boredom, encouraged camaraderie, and stabilized his people's beginnings in a foreign environment. This organized appeal to Origin and commitment to active participation came from the Edo Court Volunteer members of the Retinue who, in some instances, were descendants of Edo hierarchal lines. These loyal Elders were able to adapt the traditions and culture of centuries of interdependence in city life as well as their familiarity with functioning constituted authority to the challenges at hand.

With little difficulty, a capable and suitable candidate for the position of First Minister, Confidant, and Guardian of Access as well as Custodian of the Camp was nominated. A Minister of Finance in charge of the prince's purse, inventories, and their valuation, as well as a Minister of Works responsible for camp maintenance and construction projects was also nominated. Working in harmony with the men, the ministerial team quickly duplicated its Edo environment that produced a community ready to meet the Prince's next challenge.

On their return to the riverines in the early years of the 1480s, Portuguese merchants found a community ready for trade and the cultivation of good relations. Its resources of merchandise included peppers, elephant tusks, leopard skins, and terra-cotta. These items were desirable enough for the community to become an economically viable stop in the Lisboa ("Lisbon" in Portuguese)-São Tomé leg of the voyage from Portugal to the East Indies.

The profitable calls made Prince Iginua's Ijala the premier Portuguese trading destination on the Bight of Benin. As trading continued to grow, so did the steady accumulation of wealth in the Itsekiri homeland—first by the Prince and his community and then by the native Itsekiris. Within the exiled community, the new economic status of its members raised morale and strengthened their loyalty. It became increasingly evident that if there had been any previous or secret considerations of a return to Ubini, these were now increasingly negated by the circumstance of a newly attained affluence.

The success of the Prince was mirrored by the fleet of vessels he commissioned for the expanding commerce. His maturity and continuity were marked by the birth of his first son. At a ceremony to celebrate the event, he conferred on himself the title of Ogiame (King of the Seas). Undoubtedly, he intended to send a message indicating independence of the land-based Edo Court. He also ordered seven days of festivities to honor Olokun, the Deity of the Seas and Patron of the mission, and Ibrikimo, the Royal Guardian Land Spirit who had brought great success to the workings of the camp.

Oba Olua died in 1480, two years after he initiated and carried out the exile of his son, Prince Iginua. His successor, Oba Ozolua, was not nominated, however, until 1482 and not sworn into office until 1483. Thus Prince Iginua's absence did not materially affect the Palace wrangling that some had predicted when they supported Oba Olua's action. During the inter-regnum, no palace official had the authority or power, much less the inclination, to challenge Prince Iginua on his inaction regarding the conditions set out in Oba Olua's Proclamation of Exile.

Once Oba Ozolua was enthroned in 1483, it was not only impolitic to mention Prince Iginua by name, but his person was also generally considered irrelevant to matters in hand. The Oba established and consolidated his position. In the second decade of the Oba's reign, starting in 1493, both the increasing notoriety of Iginua's wealth, which was accrued through commercial activity with the Portuguese and stability at home, enabled Oba Ozolua to send emissaries to the Prince asking him to fulfill his obligations as set out in the Proclamation of Exile.

After repeated requests had been ignored, he threatened the Prince with action by the Edo Army. At this point, and after long consideration, the Prince answered, "The Proclamation was an agreement between my father and I in which his successors were neither named nor granted any powers." The curt reply did not please the Oba, but he was not in a position to go to the limits of his authority or powers to pursue the matter. The wrangles of the interregnum had brought the Palace into disrepute with the citizens of the kingdom. To wage war against the only Prince not involved in that situation would be an unpopular course of action.

Yet, the Oba had to show sympathy, if not empathy, with the "neglected" families of Iginua's faithful supporters. His compromise was to create an expeditionary force to engage Prince Iginua in limited military action and free his followers. He also found the proper Commander of the Force in General Ekpenede—a veteran of numerous successful campaigns. Details of the exchange between Oba Ozolua and his brother Prince Iginua were not publicized although it was common knowledge in the city that there had been discussions between both parties. In measured language, the Oba announced that discussions with Prince Iginua about his obligations, under the Proclamation of Exile, to the Court and the families of certain members of his entourage were unproductive. "Therefore, necessary steps would be undertaken to bring home the individuals concerned."

General Ekpenede was born into a family with military traditions, they lived in the Ekpenede District of the city, whose main thoroughfare was named Ekpenede Street. The general, a veteran of numerous successful campaigns, was known for the limited casualty rate among his troops and his humane treatment of the conquered. His résumé made him the ideal person for the Oba to select as Commander of the Expeditionary Force for the delicate mission of confronting Prince Iginua.

Gloom and apprehension accurately describe the mood of the Prince's men as news of the Oba's appointment of General Ekpenede to pursue and produce their leader spread through the Ijala Camp. In addition to the awe inspired by the warrior's reputation, the men could not realistically identify any aspect of combat in which there would be a credible challenge to the trained men of the Edo Army under the General's command. The men recognized that direct confrontation would be suicidal. In a flash, these loyalists visualized themselves scuttling the painstakingly nurtured and now vibrant community they had constructed. Horrified and despondent at such possible outcome, they quickly recoiled from a similarly self-destructive course of action.

But, escape for the Prince and therefore themselves was impractical given the nature of their environment. There did not appear to be an alternative to surrender!

Therefore, it was surprising to see a smiling Prince Iginua in lighthearted conversation as he came to address the people at a town meeting. The prince, whose last public display of optimism was at the city work sites before departing for Ijala, had an option that held a good chance of success. The Oba wanted him and some highly valued members of the community. They would leave the camp for the uncharted waterways and small settlements of the eastern riverines and remain there long enough to frustrate his intended captors. The Edo Military was land-conflict oriented. As such, it was without bases, personnel with adequate aquatic training or experience, and equipment essential for naval conflicts in the waterways. The crews of the Prince's merchantmen were, however, familiar with the territory and its varied conditions including the local tides from ferrying the Prince between the settlements. The Elders of one of these settlements in particular extended an open invitation for a return visit. It would be a fitting launching site for the Prince's escape into the little known water channels of the eastern riverines.

Once again, two decades after arrival at Ijala, Prince Iginua was outfitting vessels. On this occasion, though, there was no real destination and no assigned mission. He was no longer a recognized, if unofficial, envoy to the kingdom—only a fugitive from a famous warrior. After weeks of preparation and organization, Prince Iginua and his at-risk entourage embarked on their voyage into the labyrinth of the eastern riverines. For the Prince, this was the first occasion in which he left his sons and daughter without an idea of the length of his mission. Gradually, the anguish began to show on his face. The First Minister gave orders for the departure that would not be further delayed.

Concurrent with the Prince's preparations and departure into the labyrinth of waterways of the southeast riverines, General Ekpende began his methodical and deliberate mobilization of the kingdom's resources in the formation and organization of the Expeditionary Force. Under the announced auspices of the Palace, he had unrestricted access to personnel and matériel. Ekpende also activated camps for military training, especially in the context of basic physical endurance, which was necessary for a prolonged mission. Various types of transporters were built and storage facilities for equipment and smoked or dried provisions were erected. All over the contiguous city-states, military scouts shadowed Prince Iginua's likely sympathizers and reported on their movements while assuring the rulers that their territories would be used for passage only.

In 1497, because his program was fully funded and efficiently executed, the General had three companies of well equipped, trained, and disciplined foot soldiers ready to carry out the Oba's command. Following a semiofficial launching ceremony at the Palace grounds, the Expeditionary Forces set off on its mission by trekking south along the margin of the rain forest at the riverines. Its destination was a location north of the right bank of the Oeri River. The General had selected this site to establish a staging area for his forays into the riverine waterways and the Itsekiri settlement off the left bank. His intelligence had indicated this settlement sheltered the errant Prince and his Courtiers.

The Expeditionary Force quickly settled into a military base routine at Ogunu. The anticipation of a rapid conclusion of its mission provided a reason for high morale. Reconnaissance at the riverside soon, however, dampened the men's enthusiasm. A body of water more than one hundred meters wide, with unknown and hidden hazards, separated the men from an indeterminate location of the Prince amongst the myriad waterways beyond the left bank. The expanse of water exposed the limitations of their now obviously inadequate vessels that had been originally designed for small waterway campaigns.

Nonetheless, after personally assessing the situation, the General was not to be deterred by a mere natural obstacle. He quickly outlined a two-pronged strategy. With the resources at hand, he immediately initiated a psychological offensive. His scouts used their contact with Idirigbo Okotomu fishermen on the river to relay repeated threats of military action against the settlement if it persisted in providing shelter or refuge for the Prince and his men.

The General then turned his attention to the predicament created by the ferry. His plan was to provide some form of watercraft that was capable of conveying a platoon of approximately ten men to designated locations. The watercraft had to survive rough waters and the possible attempts of divers to capsize their vessels by using driftwood or other forms of floating debris as cover. The lack of a significant hardwood supply excluded construction of large vessels in the time frame of a campaign originally planned with a limited military objective.

The remaining option was to build rafts large enough to transport an envisaged number of men for specific objectives. Directions were immediately issued for the felling of the available softwood trees, hauling the lumber to the rivulets, and floating them to the riverbank to be secured with the readily available cane-reed fibers to form rafts.

Activity on the right bank and its progress in the production of readily recognized means of water transport did not go unnoticed or unreported on the left bank. This and the persistent demand for response to the threats fueled fear and uneasiness in the community. Indeed, as the ultimate prize of the unfolding drama, the Prince, because of his silence, was accused of indifference to the consequences of exposing the settlement to the might of the Edo military— very much to the discomfiture of the Elders who had pledged an open invitation to the Prince.

In the climate of fear and with evidence of a growing backlash against him, Prince Iginua asked for a private meeting with the Elders. He disclosed arrangements for the delivery of a message to the General's men. The meeting provided the opportunity to assure the community that he would not, under any circumstances, sacrifice the people or the settlement to his self-interest.

Shortly before the sun reached its zenith two days after the meeting, three boats appeared upstream from the site of operations of the General's men. When they came abreast of a waiting and anticipatory audience, they steered crosswise. In full regalia, the Prince stood up to speak. His voice rang out over the river basin.

"Hear me, Edo warriors. I speak to you today of the future and not the past with which you may not be familiar. Within seven days, our Divine Lord and my sponsor, Oklokun will visit us all; as will my guiding Land Spirit, Ibrikimo. Their visitation will end either with the devastation of your camp and your General's schemes or my departure into their realm. I hereby, without malice or rancor, commend you to their care and bid you farewell." It was an unusually brief message from the Prince that ended with his vessel pulling away into the waterways of the left bank.

There was no doubt that the meeting had been choreographed to some extent. The Prince was dramatic, if not intimidating, to the young foot soldiers of the Expeditionary Force who had only heard of a popular exiled Prince who was the subject of their mission. It may also have appeared to some that this was the swan song—a final gesture of an individual in denial of the purpose and determination of the Edo Army. Whatever message the scene or invocation was intended to convey, both are memorialized in the chronicle of the Iginua Dynasty as the last occasion on which Prince Iginua communicated with Agents of the Edo Court that had sent him adrift in the riverines. This also marked the beginning of the unusual process to nullify his indebtedness to that authority and produced the first named ruler in Itsekiriland.

At daybreak on the third day after the Prince delivered his speech on the Oeri River, the sun rose no differently than the day before. The cocks crowed early, as usual, and awakened all in the settlement. In the compounds, hens with chicks hurried hither and thither as they pecked at or picked up objects that were often beyond human vision. All seemed normal. For those who were a little more observant, the waves lapped a little farther and louder at the water's edge; the wind ruffled the leaves of the mangrove trees a little more briskly. By late afternoon, conditions changed. Cumulus clouds hid the sun from view so that it lost its brightness and much of its power. Soon, very soon, flashes of lightning were followed by the clattering and rumblings of thunder; Idirigbo Okotomu and beyond were in semidarkness.

On the right bank camp at Ogunu, grey clouds blanketed the

sky as the men hustled to take shelter in their huts from high winds. Suddenly, an endless sheet of water tumbled down on the camp. The force of the falling water leveled the structures that had survived the preceding gusts of wind, sending men running into the open spaces. As streams broke their banks and began to flood the area, the command went out for the men to abandon camp and seek shelter on higher ground.

On the riverbank, the scene was even more chaotic. Moorings not swept away by high waves were broken as their tethers of cane reeds dangled loose; logs from rafts that were torn apart drifted everywhere on the river. And then, the rains came. For three days and nights, the notorious river basin rain compounded the camp's flooding with floating debris and mud. The former streams and rivulets became waterways that carried all in their paths with them to the estuary.

It was impossible for the men to return from the comparative safety of the higher grounds of modern day Okere and Ajamimogha. Dispirited and confused, they were forced to continue huddling under trees for shelter. The equipment assembled at the riverside and the personal belongings at the camp were lost or destroyed in weather conditions that the men had never experienced or envisioned. Amid the devastation, they realized that practically speaking, their mission was at an end. Many wept.

It is no wonder that the memory of a disaster, from which they might have been spared by the early release of the Prince to their custody, nurtured a grudge against the people of Idirigbo Okotomu that was passed down through many generations.

On the left bank, the rains made a greater impression than the initial storm that seemed just like late season downpours. The fishermen who returned to the river were astounded by the extent of damage and disorder on the right bank and the amount of floating debris in the river. There were no signs of life in the makeshift dockyards. Not long thereafter, news of the devastation on the right bank reached the Idirigbo community that resulted in a rapidly initiated movement for reconciliation with the Prince.

The Elders felt vindicated in their long-held belief that Prince Iginua was sent to the riverines to be the Ruler of Idirigbo Okotomu. They quickly became his sponsors and formally asked the Prince to accept the leadership role and title of Ogbowuru. The Prince accepted the offer but asked for forbearance. He had been away from his home and not seen his family including two adolescent sons for a long time. He wanted very much to be reunited with them before assuming the title. Moreover, other personal and Ijala community affairs needed attention. As soon as these matters were attended to, he and his Court would return to the people of Idirigbo. At this stage of the discussions, the First Minister informed the audience that with the fulfillment of their long-held wishes, they should formally address the Prince as Ogiame. To assure them of the Prince's commitment to return, two members of the team remained in the settlement to help with the building of residences and other infrastructure necessary for the proper functioning of the Court.

Although the Elders were requested to be discreet about information related to Prince Iginua's departure, this was hardly the case. The crowd at the pier on the morning of his departure grew quickly. A loud "Ogiame" greeted him followed by "Farewell" and "Return soon." Of its own accord, the settlement had, except for the ceremony, installed Prince Iginua as its leader.

Looking out on the scene, a sense of satisfaction was apparent on the Prince's face. He and his loyal followers had survived a campaign mounted by the most powerful monarch in their world. As the flotilla maneuvered through the debris-laden river on its way to Ijala, it was sweet and reassuring to know that the men were returning home and not being led away to Benin City as prisoners of the General. The feeling was commonly shared as the songs and the rhythm of paddles slicing through water propelled them home.

The Rock
Prince Ijijen: The
Unheralded Prince

A t a sandbank stop the day after Prince Iginua, Ogbowuru designate, and his party left Idirigbo Okotomu in triumph, the High Priest took the Prince aside to warn him of the possibility of encountering personal grief at home. Unfortunately, based on previous experiences, the Priest's warnings could not be summarily dismissed. Various possible tragedies raced through the Prince's mind as he remained awake throughout the night. His fears were not allayed when members of his family did not join the crowd that gave him a rather subdued welcome. Visibly distraught, he hurried his way through the crowd to his residence where he was greeted solemnly by his wife and junior son. One glance that took in the entire room confirmed his greatest fears. He collapsed on the nearest resting place.

Prince Iginua, Ogiame (King of the Seas) Odihi n'ame (Prince of the Rivers) and all but installed Ogbowuru of Idirigbo Okotomu (Leader of the Legions of People of Idirigbo Okotomu), could not recover from the shock of his son's death during his absence.

An absence that was designed to divert General Ekpenede from Ijala and his family became one of parental neglect at a time when episodes of high body heat and shivering ended in uncontrolled ague and then total lifelessness. Through all the young man's suffering, his father was not there to embrace and comfort the aching body of a suffering son. Feelings of self-reproach and guilt consumed the Prince. This self-imposed burden of failure gnawed at an unexpectedly turned sensitive Prince. Refusing all entreaties to be comforted, he would soon die of a broken heart. Having received the assurance, but without assumption, of the leadership of Idirigbo Okotomu Settlement, Prince Iginua died in 1500.

During the celebrations that marked the birth of Prince Iginua's first son, the Court recognized the title of Ogiame (King of the Seas) and endorsed the adoption of the principle of male primogeniture succession. Although both sons were educated according to Edo Court and Palace traditions, it was the elder son who received particular attention with regard to Palace protocol and obligations. The unexpected successive deaths of his brother and his father brought a new dimension to Prince Ijijen's life as heir apparent.

As he began to adjust to his new status, the High Priest announced a crisis situation created by serial deaths; the circumstances of the deaths were not only unusual but might have also resulted from misdeeds or transgressions against Olokun and Ibrikimo. To uncover any such acts and assuage the Gods, if necessary, a pause devoted to special offerings and supplications was required. Thus, the priests performed their rites and submitted their offerings while the populace waited. Finally, the High Priest announced the exoneration of all the people from acts against Olokun or Ibrikimo.

After a convenient interval, the Chief Minister and other senior ministers, acting as kingmakers, pronounced Prince Ijijen successor to the title of "Ogiame." The title would be publicly conferred at his installation as Ogbowuru of Idirigbo Okotomu. Loyalists, even as they grieved, had sent word to inform the Ministers that their plans to receive and welcome Ogiame were unchanged.

The devoted and long-suffering Iginua Court had envisioned a return to a normal calendar after Prince Iginua had successfully shaken off their nemesis, General Ekpenede. Any such hopes and

21

desires were rapidly overtaken by events. A traumatic experience of the loss of its original symbol of loyalty and oneness was aggravated by the responsibility of conducting funeral rites at the internment of an Edo Prince outside the Kingdom and outside living memory. The Court had to nurture a young Prince as he learned its methods and traditions as well as the obligations and the demands on a monarch. These issues were compounded by the practical necessity to address the logistics of its own and the Prince's relocation to Idirigbo Okotomu. Despite these various pressures, it is to the Court's credit that under the leadership of the Chief Minister at a time when no established Iginua ruling lineage existed, there was no evidence of intrigue, discontent, or disintegration of its membership.

As a unit that was determined to succeed in a mission it had voluntarily undertaken more than two decades before this crisis, the Court painstakingly applied itself to the tasks before it. Prince Iginua was interred in Ijala without incident or outrage. The young Prince Ijijen was patiently tutored for his leadership role and a flotilla was assembled for the voyage to a new seat of government.

As these different endeavors took final form, the Chief Minister convened a session of the Court. When members had taken their places, he turned to Prince Ijijen. "Ogiame," he began, "many years ago we, members of this Court, started a journey with your late father with the expectation that he would one day be in your present position at the threshold of being proclaimed a Ruler. Things have turned out differently as we can see. But not that much! On behalf of us all present, I pledge to you the same loyalty and devotion that was Iginua's and charge you now to be the Head of this Court. Congratulations."

The loyal members of the Iginua Court had publicly cast their lot with a new leader, an unheralded Prince who would assume the role by force of circumstance. Prince Ijijen's mind wandered for a brief moment to his early and even recent life—a happy and apparently unburdened boyhood and adolescence—that had been abruptly redirected by unexpected events. *"What a parallel to my late father's life's course?"* he asked himself as his attention returned to the Court. Then, briefly contemplating the Chief Minister's charge, he gathered his thoughts and, seemingly at no loss for words, accepted the challenge of his new status. He thanked the Chief Minister, the High Priest, and other members of the Court for their graciousness, patience, and kindness during his tutelage as well as their pledge of allegiance and loyalty. He asked that he be joined in supplications to Olokun and Ibrikimo to extend to him the goodness and protection showered on his father. He ended with a statement: "With life's uncertainty so remarkably illustrated in our lives recently, I solemnly make this request of the Court. It is my wish that at my life's end, it will direct without equivocation that my remains be brought back to Ijala to be interred beside those of my father and my brother so that the three of us shall be together through eternity."

All divisions of the departure program came to ready during the final days before departure. Heavy luggage had been shipped ahead not only for convenience, but also as a reassurance to the loyalists of Idirgbo Okotomu. Information on the timetable for departure had been given to all involved in the relocation process.

The Prince's conveyance was visibly, though not ostentatiously, fitted to provide a measure of comfort and was distinguished by an escort of specially manned vessels that led the body of the flotilla. In the final moments, however, it was the personal or emotional elements that were most demanding of the voyagers. Separation can be bittersweet. So it was on that day in the year 1500 as each vessel was boarded.

After two decades or more of calling Ijala its base, with all that the settlement represented as in associations, community, successes, and even survival, leaving was truly bittersweet for the Court. Absent from the midst of many movements in that departure scene and resting not far from it was the former symbol of their unity, devotion, loyalty, and love who should have been leading this voyage to glory. And Prince Ijijen? His face reflected the certainty that this was the voyage before the final one that would return him to the side of the first Ogiame for all time. In that final moment, when most eyes were filled with tears, the flotilla pulled away from the shoreline en route to another beginning.

Harvesting the riverines has always been an integral component of the local economy. While the main waterways served as a communication highway system, their tributaries and associated creeks were playgrounds with individually defined limits for both adults and children to swim and frolic. Their use as the community's ceremonial highway now awaited the Prince and his entourage as they wound their way to Idirigbo Okotomu. An hour or more before they arrived at the Oeri River, rhythmic drumbeats floated in the air as if to reassure them. The flotilla made its final turn into the river to take advantage of the morning tide and was greeted by an extravagantly colorful scene. Numerous vessels gleaming in the sunshine and decked with colorful banners were massed midstream. As the leading boat of the flotilla approached, they broke into a formation of escorts for the Prince.

Prince Ijijen faced serious challenges when he became the first Ogbowuru. His father, Prince Iginua, had been a legend at Idirigbo Okotomu in his own lifetime. Although General Ekpenede and his men had given up on their mission, they nonetheless remained resentful of the Elders of the settlement. Thus, in addition to the tasks and responsibilities of leadership, Ogbowuru Ijijen had to demonstrate his worthiness to succeed his father as well as endeavor to reduce the simmering tension between both banks. Therefore, soon after his installation, the Ogbowuru started a peace initiative. Employing General Ekpende's tactics, he sent word about his hopes through fishermen to the right bank settlements. The new leader held out his hand for peace. Born and raised outside of the Edo

Kingdom long after his father's departure from Ubini Palace, he was not involved in any dispute with that institution. His desire was to live and lead Idirigbo Okotomie peaceably and without conflict.

The upper echelons of the Expeditionary Force ignored the Ogbowuru's overtures just as they had with Idirgbo Okotomu's Elders after their rejection of the request to surrender Prince Iginua and members of his Retinue. Indeed, in their pursuit of a "cold shoulder" policy toward the Elders, they regularly preferred the hinterland to the settlement across the river for seeking spouses. The rank and file, however, acted contrarily. The right bank grew into a diverse and predominantly Itsekiri speaking population that was more favorable to peaceful coexistence. This changing demographic gradually undermined the hostility of the leaders so that their silence was ultimately ignored and deemed benign on both banks of the river. In an effort to positively influence the situation, the Ogbowuru sent the Idirigbo Okotomu fishermen on their errand.

As the possibility of conflict in the river basin receded, the Ogbowuru and his Court conducted their affairs, participated in obligatory community events, and introduced Edo Calendar ceremonies and commemorative feasts in a peaceful and sensitive manner. The growing popularity of the leader, partly resulting from these activities and the happy event of a son two years after arriving at Idirigbo, Oktomu prompted advisers to consider action directed toward a broader recognition and acceptance in the remaining Itsekiri settlements. Although unenthusiastic about the details of plans pursued by the Senior Ministers, he finally agreed to a feast to commemorate Prince Iginua's original adoption of Ogiame as his premier title. Three days of carefully timed meetings took place between various forms of merriment. However, it became apparent that despite its overwhelming social success, the underlying objective of the celebrations remained elusive. The guest Elders

25

did not commit their communities to any relationship that would recognize the Ogbowuru as the leader.

The setback to the Minister's attempt to widen the Ogbowuru's acceptance could be attributed, in large measure, to the state of affairs in Edo Kingdom. Through numerous channels, it was known in the settlements that Oba Ozolua was unhappy with the outcome of General Ekpenede's mission, but the Oba's future actions were unknown when he died in 1504. Oba Esigie, who succeeded Oba Ozolua, was still an enigma. This uncertain situation at the Edo Palace provided the Elders of the settlements a plausible excuse to remain uncommitted.

By the time Prince Ijijen died in Idirigbo Okotomu in 1525, a quarter of a century after that community proclaimed him Ogbowuru and the first hereditary ruler in Itsekiriland, he and his ministers had restored the fractured Iginua Court's reputation of orthodox Edo Court protocol, practicality, and successful negotiations. The Court's decision to include some events and celebrations relevant to the lives of the local populace fostered a bond that withstood stresses in the society during his lifetime. His self-assuredness, coupled with a compromising nature as well as the willingness to function in the larger interest of the people without overreaching, contributed to a successful reign and provided the grounds for the undisputed acceptance of his son, Prince Irame, as successor.

As these accomplishments, and many more, were celebrated during Prince Ijijen's last rites, one was overlooked. That accomplishment was his response to the traumatic experience of the sequential deaths of his brother (the heir apparent) and his father, which unexpectedly propelled him to inherit what was only a fledgling of a ruling line. Notwithstanding his prior tendency toward, or vision of, a life outside the Court, the unheralded Prince dutifully and without excuses accepted the challenge. His dedication, attitude, and willingness to work with the seniors of the Court, with whom he previously had only cursory relations, ensured the survival of the Dynasty. Even as his remains traversed the waterways of the riverines to its final destination as he had requested, he was enhancing the Iginua mystique. When laid to rest beside his father, the act would be the precedent that established Ijala as the necropolis of the Iginua Dynasty.

Birth of The Warri (Itsekiri) Kingdom Ojoluwa Court's Triumph: Union of Settlements

The defeat of the International Crusade at the Battle of Nicopolis in 1396 effectively ended Western efforts to win back control of the Holy Land from the Turks who captured Jerusalem in 1244. The disappointing performance of the army has been ascribed to numerous factors which include wrangling and rivalry among the rulers of the donor north European Dukedoms; inept military command, lack of discipline of the foreign knights and their footsoldiers in the field as well as ever changing or numerous objectives. It is relevant to also observe that the donors' inability to recover their outlay on the crusade put them in financial straits.

In contrast, successive strong leadership figures, a well defined objective and a common purpose to defeat the occupiers characterized and energized the National Crusade. Peter II's 1212 victory over Almohades in Spain was followed by other victories in Cordoba and Valencia in 1236 and 1248 respectively. Only the beleaguered Granada in Southern Spain and isolated spots in Portugal remained under control of the Moors after these victories. In the era of relative peace that followed, the Reconquest restored sovereignty and Christianity to the nationals of the Iberian Peninsula. With sovereignty they took control of its wealth and Portugal began her expansion of Europe's trade with North Africa to West Africa and beyond.

Restored Christianity underpinned by the nationals' wealth ensured the continuous flow of funds to Rome in the form of Church taxes and sales of indulgences. The resultant and inarguably enhanced status of the successful Reconquista nations was recognized and manifested in the mid-century Papal bulls of the years between 1450 and 1460.

For example, The King of Portugal was assigned exclusive trade and missionary rights in Africa and east of Africa that successive sovereigns exercised to various degrees. In 1510, six years into the reign of Oba Esigie, the King of Portugal, Dom Manuel, expanded his nation's solely commercial activity in the West Coast of Africa to include diplomatic and religious missions. A diocese of West Africa extending from Cape Verde to Mozambique was created with a bishopric on the island of São Tomé. An Ambassador was accredited to the legendary African State of Benin. That year, Ambassador Pirez and a team of missionaries arrived in Benin City to establish a presence designed principally as an outpost of Christendom in the Roman Catholic strategy of stemming the advance of Islam south of the Sahara Desert.

The formalities of exchange of Ambassadors were hardly completed when concerns surfaced about a surrogate uprising in the River Niger's left bank city of Idah. The escalation of the uprising threatened Agenegbode, the market town and Northern Gateway to the Empire nestled in the foothills of the Kurkuruku Mountains.

The uprising eventually required intervention by the Edo Army. Oba Esigie led the army, with some members of the Portuguese missionary team in attendance, one hundred miles to the Idah battlefield in a successful campaign that established a Pax Esigie. The Oba was the only holder of that office in living memory to fulfill the cherished and demanding obligation of personally and successfully leading the army to battle. He was welcomed home with awe, gratitude, and appropriate ceremonies. Omo n' Oba Esigie was truly Uku Akpolokpolo—"The First and Highest One!"

In the glorious early days of his reign, Oba Esigie made land grants to the missionaries in recognition and appreciation of their participation in the Idah Campaign. He also directed, according to Ambassador Pirez, his son and two noblemen to become Christians and attend Portuguese language classes. Even though the Oba did not participate in these activities, the directives were not popular at Court. As the rituals and various requirements of the Roman Catholic Church became better known, opposition to further personal involvement by the Prince mounted. In 1522, the missionaries were informed that their form of religious worship was unacceptable. The beliefs and rites that had sustained the Oba, his Court, and the Kingdom from time beyond the limits of memory would neither be abandoned nor exchanged for a foreign faith that did not accept the primacy and secrecy of those tenets.

Later that year, a fleet of Portuguese merchantmen sailed into the vicinity of Idirigbo Okotomu. This signaled the decision to allow the Edo Kingdom to pursue its own self-sufficient, self-directed Renaissance and cultural achievements outside of European influence for another three hundred years. It also provided a new focus of Portuguese interest on the West African Coast.

The stability and security of what might be called Pax Esigie in the Edo Kingdom and Empire extended to the riverines even if it was by default arising from the Oba's neglect. Ogbowuru Ijijen's rule lasted a quarter of a century which was the first half of Oba Esigie's reign. This guaranteed the survival of the Iginua lineage and witnessed the reemergence of Iginua's son as the premier Portuguese trading partner on the Bight of Benin upon the Portuguese's return in 1522. Ogbowuru Irame, Iginua's grandson, significantly expanded the trade by consolidating his father's achievements and bringing increased commercial activity to the riverines. Success was visibly reflected in the lifestyle of the

Itsekiris. The mooted question was when would this emerging Kingdom's envied trading position be challenged? The challenge came early in Ogbowuru Irame's reign when men from neighboring tribes staged attacks on innocent Itsekiris. Apparently, the leader had anticipated such a confrontation. Out of public view, he built a naval force of war canoes manned by trained armed men. The rapid response successfully removed any threat to the trade and provided assurances of safety to the Portuguese merchants while guaranteeing the stability and security of Idirigbo Okotomu and the riverines. Ogbowuru Irame's success made a great impression on the Elders of the other Itsekiri settlements and set in motion discussions that eventually resulted in the creation of the Itsekiri Kingdom in his lifetime.

In 1550, after the death of Ogbowuru Irame, Prince Ojoluwa assumed office and inherited a realm that extended from the Edo Kingdom in the north to the Atlantic Ocean in the south and included most of the riverines that existed only in the mind of his great grandfather at the time of his exile.

In the new Kingdom, the Itsekiri-Yoruba ethnic majority retained its traditional ways of life and secured the internal autonomy of individual settlements. Equally significant, it acquired a symbol of unity as in "Ogiame, King of the Seas" and a leader, the "Olu," to whom the Itsekiri-Yoruba pledged allegiance.

The apparent losers in the negotiations to create a union were the original Iwere Royalists of Idirigbo Okotomu. At considerable risk, they defied General Ekpenede by shielding Prince Iginua and then proceeded to invite Prince Ijijen to be their first leader or Ogbowuru. Because, or as a result of historic gesture, Idirigbo Okotomu remained the seat of the Olu. For this honor, however, it became known as Ode-Itsekiri, and their sacrifice and loyalty to the now acceptable Monarchy would not be further acclaimed. Finally, as a people, the Iwere's would be denied recognition and asked to change their identity.

Rather painfully, all these concessions were to be made with the tacit approval of the Court. In some measure, however, events occurring simultaneously with the forging of the Union undermined the supposedly well-laid strategy of the majority.

The invigorated and profitable Portuguese trade under the Ogbowuru's patronage made Okotomu the market place of the riverines. Its people, the Iweres, were the primary middlemen. For the Portuguese merchants, Iwere was much less a phonetic challenge than Idirigbo Okotomu and easily corrupted to Oeri as it came to be known in Portuguese documents, maps, and log books. The balance of recognition shifted in favor of the Iweres as they became increasingly identified with the trade and its articles locally and far afield. The Itsekiris gradually changed as Oeri became the name of the port, the Kingdom and its people.

The Ogbowuru's Court immediately began to make arrangements for the installation ceremony of a ruler of the new Itsekiri Kingdom. The site for celebration of this unique occasion was, as previously indicated Ode Itsekiri; previously known as Idirgbo Okotomu and which was the home settlement of the Iweres.

The occasion was to start the process of merging the people of the various settlements into one nation under the Olu.

It became the forerunner of many such gatherings at which the call for oneness, higher devotion, and accomplishments will ring out to all Itsekiris as follows.

Omi Iwere dede/Aghan Suun?
Eneh suun o----oh!

At Itsekiri gatherings, the call for higher devotion and accomplishments ring out.

Iwere children everywhere/Are you asleep?
No! We are not asleep at all!

Itsekiris were Iwere!

The Celebration

Many of the celebrants arrived in large canoes; others made the journey in small canoes whose edges just cleared the water surface and remained afloat only by the untiring efforts of designated bailers. They arrived tired, but certainly not exhausted or in bad disposition. They had made good time by using the tides to float their crafts on the way to an experience of a lifetime—citizens of a new nation anxious to become part of history. The feasting and dancing commenced without any missteps; the organizing fingerprints of succeeding Iginua Courts could be recognized. Menu at Idirigbo Okotomu Celebration.

Oje Owowo:

1. Igbagba: to ni eja-mimi to ni ide, biri eja gbigbe

2. Epuru

3. Ogolo Ale

Biri:

4. Egun
Ekpo Itsekiri
Ataghn ta seh,
Matata ta sohn
Koko ta seh,
Orusun ta sohn

Tidbits included:
Ukuaka

Breakfast:

1. Pepper soup of spices cooked with fresh fish or crayfish and dried smoked fish

2. Pottage of pepper soup, green plantain, koko yam, yam

3. Aioli of spices

Accompanied by:

4. Cassava starch
Pure palm oil
Roasted or oiled:
Green plantain
Sweet potato
Koko yam and yam

Steamed corn cakes with crayfish and dried fish

Feniyen	Farina
Ikolo	Wood larvae (from palm wine trees)
Eja biri jole gbigbe	Dried fish and shrimp
Esin ta sohn	Roast pig

Oje osohn biri Oje aleh:

Main meals of:

1. (a) Owo

1. (a) Local pottage (yams, plantain, smoked and dried fish)

(b) Owo-Isemi To ni Dibri, Ide Shara

(b) Local pottage with beans and fresh seafood of crab, lobster

2. Obien Enye To ni Ekpiye, Igugun, biri Imekpe.

2. Fresh palm pulp soup or banga soup with fish (tilapia, catfish) and periwinkle

3. Igbagba

Pepper soup with:

(a) Igbogiri

(a) Ground melon seed

(b) Ofafo

(b) Okro

Biri:

As well as:

Egun

Cassava starch

Egun—obobo

Cassava starch incorporating ripe plantain

Ataghn, Orusun

Green plantain, yams

Emo:

Drinks:

Emi Itsekiri

Fresh palm wine

Schnapp

Schnapps

On the seventh day of the revelry, Prince Ojoluwa was led to the Settlement Square before his people and the kingmakers. After invocations to his ancestors and entreaties that he would uphold the honor of his predecessors by responsibly discharging the duties of his office, he was anointed Olu Ojoluwa and proclaimed "Ogiame."

The reaction to the proclamation was a spontaneous, "Suo-o-oh," which translates to forever. This very apt and overwhelmingly appropriate response combined with "Ogiame," "Suo-o-oh," was immediately adopted as the official acknowledgement or salutation of an Olu's appearance before an audience.

After this exhilarating sequence of events, Olu Ojoluwa was entertained to an exhibition of rowing and acrobatics synchronized to the rhythm of beats from drums mounted in fully decked vessels. This was the first Coronation Regatta and a trailblazer of requests to the Olu (by future rulers of Nigeria) for Itsekiris to present what was regarded as the best choreographed entertainment in West Africa.

On any scale of measuring success and merit, the solemnity and awe of the public anointment of Ogiame, Olu Ojoluwa, Monarch of Iwere Kingdom was the highlight of the seven days of the inaugural festivities. The Coronation Regatta that showcased vessels manned by skilled and disciplined personnel, similar to those his father Olu Irame deployed to defeat and dissipate, "would be pirates on the riverine waterways." was a close second attraction. Indeed, it was their successful naval campaigns, employing similar vessels that secured free movement on the riverine waterways and convinced the Elders of the majority ethnic Yoruba-Itsekiri settlements that it was in their best interest to accept leadership modeled in the Edo tradition. The resulting local stability enabled the new Olu to make continued expansion of the Portuguese trade his priority even as news of the death of his iconic distant uncle, Oba Esigie, after whom he named his son, reached Oeri.

A Secure Kingdom, Trade, and Religion Prince Sebastian: Warri's First Christian Student and Merchant Prince

Calls at Oeri by merchant vessels from which Portuguese priests of the Augustine Order disembarked and remained on shore for varying periods of time began before 1560. The priests' visits depended on the unpredictable arrivals of vessels and their priests' tolerance of mosquitoes—the ubiquitous nuisance of the riverines. The motive for the sojourns was not difficult to identify. Concern was growing in Lisbon. After forty years, no replacement had been made for the abandoned Edo outpost. Olu Ojoluwa encouraged the stay of the priests but was noncommittal to the Christian message.

After Olu Ojoluwa's death in 1570, however, his son, Olu Esigie, was more accommodating. Although he did not convert to Christianity, he gave permission for his son, Prince Eyomasan, to start lessons in the Portuguese language and to be baptized with the name Sebastian. Olu Esigie's decisions and actions in this matter may be deemed pragmatic in light of the economic situation of the Kingdom even if he was aware, as he must have been, of the historic precedent of such action. However, it can also be appreciated that the circumstances of a similar Edo decision by Oba Esigie in 1520 and his Court's reaction thereafter were different. The Edo Court and Kingdom had tradition, powerful institutions, and importantly visible, if silent, physical structures. These were constant reminders of a compelling and undeniable heritage. However, no such corresponding restraints were at hand to prevent or, in the future, annul the Oeri decisions.

Prince Sebastian

"First" in this chapter's title was used here only relatively in the context of engaging in European or Western education and transactions. The Edo Palace and Court nurtured educators and students many centuries before Europe became intrigued with the existence of Benin. In Ambassador Duarte Pires's 1516 letter to his monarch, Dom Manuel I of Portugal (1469–1516), he acknowledged the existence of indigenous scholastic traditions. Referring to the Palace students of the missionaries in Benin City, Pires wrote: "They learnt how to read and did it well." That tradition of learning continued into the Iginua Court.

In 1580 Oeri, as with the Palace students of Benin City 1516, Prince Eyomasan so impressed his priest-tutors with his enthusiasm and achievements, despite the unpredictably of their availability that they unanimously recommended that he should have formal schooling. Because of the practical implications relating to palace residence tréaditions, the Olu did not initially sanction or subscribe to this novel idea. However, over a period of time and following numerous pledges and assurances from visiting priests, Olu Esigie relented and granted permission for his son's sojourn to a foreign country.

The highlands that extend from the Central African Republic to the Northeastern States of what is now the Federal Republic of Nigeria attain a majestic stature in the Cameroun Republic. The Massif Adamoua Highlands straddles the country from east to west, north of the Central Province. At its western end, it yields to the Camerounaise dorsale which reaches south to the Atlantic

Seaboard of the Southwest Province. On a clear day, from the fisherman's market at Limbe, formerly known as Victoria, one can view the highest peak of the highlands—if not of Africa west of Mount Kilimanjaro. The Cameroun Mountain, close but not threatening, can be seen as a giant blue barrier reaching well into the sky. Offshore in the shrimp-laden waters, numerous small islands comprise the northernmost of clusters (Bioko, São Tomé e Príncipe, Annabon, and St. Helena) strewn as a discernible extrapolation of the Camerounaise Range in the mid and south Atlantic Ocean.

São Tomé, the seat of government of the tropical island cluster that is now the Democratic Republic of São Tomé e Príncipe, lies just north of the imaginary geographic line known as the Equator. Like the Cameroun Republic with which this cluster was most probably continuous before the cataclysmic cleavage of the primeval African landmass that may have created the Americas. São Tomé's volcanic origins bestow on it a unique terrain of universally fertile land with forest hills and mountains. High altitude lakes, and waterfalls cascade into rivers and streams of narrow coastal lowlands and onto the shoreline where the sea gently laps on the beautiful black volcanic rocks or crashes into some fathomless abyss locally known as "throats."

The capital city of the Democratic Republic of São Tomé e Principe is São Tomé , located at the northeastern tip of the island of the same name. A bay that forms the city's natural harbor has its own outlet sentinel of mini-islands that protect it from the swirls of the Atlantic Ocean. It is the island's main, if not only seaport. It is also the administrative, cultural, and commercial center that boasts a large vibrant central African mainland type of market. Plantations situated south of the capital city include Monte Café, with its famed and highly prized Café Arabica coffee crop and an extensive oil palm facility that caters for local needs. Mountainous forestlands are renowned for the varied fauna of foxes, wild boar, and antelopes, as well as falcons, and eagles. One spectacular mountain has a table top peak that is often hidden by low lying clouds and the challenge of conquering its vertical face has spawned a mountaineering cult among young affluent Asians and Europeans.

In 1584, this island, known as Paradise on the Equator, was the destination of a Portuguese merchant vessel. With the adolescent Prince Eyomasan/Prince Sebastian aboard, it sailed from Oeri—barely one hundred years after Prince Iginua his great, great grandfather arrived in the riverines. During his first excursion outside the riverines, the voyage to São Tomé exposed the Prince to fascinating changes of scenery. The familiar mangrove wetlands with Itsekiri settlements on the banks of the waterways soon gave way at Ugborodo to the sandy Atlantic shoreline of the Bight of Benin. At this junction of land and sea, fishermen fished or mended their nets. The ten days or so of sailing on an unending expanse of rolling waves of water seemed longer than that. Finally, the hills and mountains of São Tomé, looking majestic to a youngster born and raised on the flat banks of a narrow waterway, appeared on the horizon as the merchantman vessel made its way to São Tomé harbor.

Seated in the ferry boat, the Prince cast a glance back at the vessel. For almost two weeks, he had been a ward amongst busy and sometimes distant strangers to whose lifestyle he barely related. During the daylight hours, he was an awed witness to the passing world of nature's wonders in the quiet between the bustle of the crew's chores and lonesome cabin musings. At night, he sat in the soft light of the moon and stars that bathed the decks and the sea. At the jetty, he stepped ashore into the arms of priests and parishioners waiting to welcome the young Christian student who had come to live amongst them.

Prince and Scholar, Apprentice and Merchant

It was evident from his performance at the 1586 Nativity Festivities held in the São Tomé Cathedral School that Prince Sebastian had surpassed the most optimistic academic expectations of his tutors. He read and sang the Portuguese scripts flawlessly and spoke the language fluently. His competence extended to other areas of study that included numbers, weights, measures, and valuation skills.

Olu Esigie was kept informed of his son's progress through oral reports. The Prince's letters were delivered and translated by officers of merchantmen making calls at Oeri. Reports of the Prince's success, though impressive enough to dispel any suggestions of truancy, generated grumblings with undertones of jealousy. These included complaints of his time spent away from Court as he acquired foreign knowledge that was unlikely to be of practical use on his return. A phony controversy was kept alive by the circulating news of betrothals of the Prince's contemporaries. It is uncertain how much Olu Esigie was influenced by the controversy, but he ordered the Prince's return and an end to his schooling days in 1587.

The parable of the prodigal son is the parent's ultimate emotional and material reaction to an offspring's homecoming. For a fisherman's son who survives a storm, a returning war hero, or a daughter who has been separated from her family due to marriage, the anxiety of anticipation preceding the feverish preparations and presentations that culminate in that enveloping embrace are universally constant. A feasting and emotional reunion marked the 1587 yuletide homecoming, hosted by Olu Esigie, his Court, and Household for the returning Prince wearing a Camissa—a form of Portuguese dress shirt that became a popular Itsekiri apparel.

As the celebrations were in progress, Prince Sebastian realized how much would be expected of him. Olu Esigie indicated that in addition to his increasing responsibilities at Court, he wanted his son to become immediately and actively involved in various aspects of the Portuguese trade. Priests sought out Prince Sebastian to discuss the procurement of a site for the construction of a place of worship. His mother encouraged the early choice of a bride. Within a few weeks of homecoming, the threads of his future agenda were identified.

The Prince impressed everyone, including members of the Court who had expressed reservations about his sojourn abroad. With enthusiasm and diligence, he had attended to the aspects of the workings of the Portuguese trade assigned to him by his father. Prior to leaving home in 1584, he was not at an age when these attributes could be displayed. But watching him at work now, it was not difficult to see that the excellent reports from São Tomé Cathedral School were well earned. His knowledge of Portuguese, an asset that enhanced his credibility with the foreign merchants, enabled him to respond quickly and adequately to requests for improvements. For example, by making physical modifications to the warehouse and cataloging local and foreign merchandise with assignment of equivalent values he facilitated and streamlined the bartering process— the basics of the trade. The success of his various undertakings in trade was reflected in a remark two centuries later when other European traders identified Oeri as the "barter location" upstream from the Benin River.

Aside from the trade, the introduction of religious teachings and celebrations of Mass—ushered in by a new phase of his relations with St. Augustini Order of Priests—brought the latter more into the daily life of the community. When the christening of Dom Domingos, son of Prince Sebastian and grandson of Olu Esigie was performed in 1589, neither objection nor outcry was heard from the populace or the Court. Prince Sebastian's Christian faith and education transformed the Kingdom's passive acknowledgement and accommodation of the Portuguese traders to one of acceptance and even the adoption of their religion, language, and lifestyle.

Portuguese names of trade and household items such as *Oro* (gold), *esete* (plate), *kuyere* (spoon), *milho imiyo* (corn), and *sabatu* (shoes) crept into the Itsekiri vocabulary. Everyone was aware of the pending erection of *santoni*—the Saint Anthony compound that would ensure the continued presence of Saint Augustini priests.

Prince Eyomasan succeeded his father, Olu Esigie, as the first Christian Itsekiri Ruler—Olu Sebastian, or Olu Atrorongboye, in 1597. His interests outside of his Court responsibilities included a dedication to his religious faith, Portuguese literature, and a strong desire for his children, particularly the heir Dom Domingos, to be educated in the Portuguese tradition.

His relations with the priest community had evolved from a boyhood of school age with occasional tutoring and through a wardship of the São Tomé Mission to his present status as a father, ruler, and advocate for the causes of the priests. After years of bonding with the priests, he now had an association that transcended just the memories of prior kindnesses. In the year of his coronation, their relations reached a significant milestone when Olu Sebastian and Dom Domingos, Prince of Oeri, were hosts to Francisco de Vila Nova, the Bishop of São Tomé.

The Bishop was particularly impressed with the Olu's enthusiasm and his work to advance Christianity in Oeri, which was the only location on the West Coast of Africa where he was sympathetically received. On his return to São Tomé, the Bishop wrote to the King of Portugal seeking his help in acquiring funds needed for the expansion of Santoni, the Saint Anthony community, to include a monastery and cathedral. King Philip III of Spain was sympathetic to Bishop Nova's request. It was, in his view, the long sought for replacement of the failed pursuit of a Christian outpost in Benin City. He agreed to the Bishop's suggestion that "those who farmed the taxes of São Tomé from the lucrative ivory trade of the Congo should send priests to the King of Oeri and be remunerated with licenses to trade in slaves in his territory, provided that the King of Oeri's subjects were exempt from the trade." It was anticipated that over a number of years sufficient funds would be generated to build the compound. As a reminder of the approval of the project by King Philip, the Escravos (Slave) River still retains its then functional name five centuries later!

Olu Sebastian's faith and his aspirations for the Saint Anthony Cathedral and Monastery were not the only subjects of interest he shared with the São Tomé Bishopric and with King Philip. At the age of ten, Prince Dom Domingos was speaking, reading, and writing in Portuguese. His level of education, because of what was in effect, home schooling by his father and visiting priests, was equivalent to the highest level attained in São Tomé. This did not go unnoticed by the Bishop on his visit.

Some individuals had reservations about the suggestion of sending one of such a tender age, even if he appeared as a demonstrably high achiever, to a distant foreign land to be educated. There was, however, the possibility that in the absence of further challenges or adequate supervision at home, the same high achiever risked becoming bored and frustrated. It would not be a quickly made decision. From 1597 to 1599, Olu Sebastian pondered the situation.

But a year later, one hundred years after the death of Prince Iginua at Ijala; the anointment of Prince Ijijen as the Ogbowuru of Idirigbo Okotomu, and the substantive launching of the Iginua Dynasty, Olu Sebastian announced that Prince Dom Domingos, his son and heir, would be educated in Portugal.

Dom Domingos in Portugal—at Seats of Higher Learning

It was mostly the best of times for Dom Domingos as preparations for his departure progressed toward completion. He was excited that his expectations for further studies in his father's footsteps, nourished through years of association with tutor-priests and close learning relations with his father and mentor, was now a reality. He engrossed himself with youthful enthusiasm in the briefings, outfitting sessions, and Mass celebrations held over time to equip and familiarize him with the Portuguese way of life. He was also, understandably, supported and encouraged by the Court and people who had benefited from Olu Sebastian's pioneering sojourn in São Tomé .

All seemed to go well until the last outfitting session. The Prince was presented with two empty wooden trunks that his father had retained for more than a decade upon his return from São Tomé. At that moment, which signaled the irrevocability of the Prince's assignment, a mother's sobbing muffled all other sounds in the room. As movements of the conditioned reflex to remove her began, Olu Sebastian raised his hand and looked in the direction of his son. With not a word uttered between father and son, the Prince hurried into his mother's arms, embraced her, and let his head rest on her bosom as his tears and his mother's falling tear drops bathed his face.

This incident at the final outfitting session certainly was not an epiphany, but it did expose a toll on his mother. The Prince's deportment thereafter showed more tenderness and graciousness toward those who had nursed, cared, and continued to love him. The circumstances of that occasion, and its emotional impact, jostled for eminence in his consciousness with the almost euphoric expectations of a distant destination that held promises of unlimited access to knowledge and to new intellectual and social challenges, sans family relations or peers who, until now, had supported him. But as his departure approached, the Prince's behavior suggested that any possible or nascent mental conflict had been resolved during this period of time between the two experiences. An interval that would end with a voyage on the high seas with their heaving waves; also of blue skies and unforgettable sunsets. Sunsets, of a golden sun sitting on the shimmering waters of the western horizon, that change imperceptibly into ethereal moonlight awash decks of a carrier pressing forward and homeward in the silence of the night.

The individual lines of communication that existed between São Tomé Bishopric and Oeri on the one hand and the same Bishopric and King Philip on the other, had been joined to explore the feasibility of the ecclesiastic proposal for Olu Sebastian's Christian community. The King was drawn into the discussion after Bishop Francisco de Vila's visit to Oeri in 1597. In just over three years, Olu Sebastian, to his credit, exploited it to initiate and achieve a positive and beneficial decision on his son's education in Portugal. In 1600, one of King Philip's ships of the lucrative Lisboa to Congo Sea Passage arrived in Oeri. Dom Domingos, Prince of Oeri and son of Olu Sebastian (first Christian ruler of the Oeri Kingdom), boarded the ship for his voyage. The ship's call provided posterity with a window into the person and accomplishments of Olu Eyomosan alias Olu Sebastian. Dom Domingos carried with him a letter for King Phillip which expressed his father's wish that he should study and be instructed in European ways so that he might help his father in the conversion of his people (to which he was paying great attention) and in the Government of the Kingdom. The King was asked to assist and supervise the Prince's education as he thought best.

The personal relationships between the Portuguese King, one of his bishops and Olu Sebastian, King of the Oeri during the last decade of the sixteenth century was probably unique. It was, as we have seen also instrumental in accomplishing the remarkable feat of educating an African boy Prince in Portugal from 1600 to 1609. Before describing Don Domingo's accomplishments and relationships in Portugal, it is interesting if not informative to look at an earlier Portuguese royal personage who became an historic world figure. This individual's persistence in the endeavor that established the wider intercourse between Portugal and West Africa that we have narrowed down to personal relationships is important in our story. That intercourse in no small measure helped to determine the fate of the Iginua Dynasty.

Prince Henry the Navigator, third son of King John I of Portugal, concluded early in life that succession to his father's throne was only a remote possibility and that his personal financial security lay in his finding treasure. The realization unexpectedly came into focus in 1415. His father's navy and army had captured the North African port of Ceuta. This was in reprisal to Arab raids on the Algarve Coast to capture Portuguese women for sale in the lucrative white slave markets of Muslim North Africa.

Fortunately, all the King's sons survived the campaign. For Prince Henry, the significant aspect of the conquest was his observation that Ceuta was also the Mediterranean terminus for Muslim caravans that brought slaves and gold across the Sahara Desert for eventual sale in Europe. The Prince reasoned that treasure could be gained by hugging the North African Coast to the then unknown and distant West Africa. His strategy was to bypass the caravan Arab middlemen and the Sahara Desert, allowing him to bring the gold and slaves of Sub-Saharan Africa directly to Europe.

Europe's economic strait at the beginning of the fifteenth century made any suggestion for attaining wealth, particularly if it originated from nobility, worthy of support. This atmosphere, as well as the stability and common safety created in Portugal by King John and his capable General of the Army (Second Constable) Nuno Alvarez Pereira, enabled Prince Henry to live on the Southern Coast of Portugal (Algarve). He founded *vila do infante* (town of the Prince) and established a center for sea operations at nearby Lagos and its natural harbor.

Prince Henry never personally tested his thesis or proposal, but he brought method to his project and thus earned his title: The Navigator. He began by modifying the existing Portuguese ships (caravels). Triangular lateen sails, which were common on Arab coastal vessels and tacked against the wind, were installed. This made the handling of caravels independent of the direction of the wind. Then, with great organizational skills, he recruited or sponsored crews from Lagos to sail the caravels on voyages along the North African Coast in search of Africa's treasures.

Starting in 1415, the Prince's vessels set sail for his El Dorado by hugging the then-known African coastline. For many years, thereafter they returned empty to Lagos; each empty vessel represented failure to reach the Prince's goals of riches. Undeterred, Prince Henry made and updated maps by working with and listening to his sailors. In 1434, one Captain Gil Eanes addressed the hazards encountered at the headland of Cape Bojador, just south of modern day Morocco. "Fearsome currents and high winds which prevented further progress along the Coast," he noted, "could be overcome by going out to sea beyond the sight of land." The triangular lateen sails of his vessels were then able to tack to more favorable winds and propel him south.

By accepting and adopting Captain Eanes's report for his fleet,

Prince Henry's vision of reaching the far side of the Sahara Desert by sea became a practical possibility. By the year 1443, Portuguese sailors had reached present day Mauritania, south of Western Sahara where, it is said, they later built a powerful fort. Beginning in 1444, according to European historians, dozens of vessels left Prince Henry's port of Lagos each year bound for South Saharan Africa.

In 1452, the first real results were realized in the form of shipments of slaves and gold. The quantity of gold delivered across the seas by Europeans without reliance on overland Muslims permitted the minting of Portugal's first ever gold coin that was aptly called the cruzados.

Prince Henry had found his treasure. After heading Portugal's School of the Navy, he retired as the Duke of Viseu and died in Porto in 1460. Gradually, *vila do infante* and Lagos lost their respective residential and commerce premier positions to northern locations. The new Lisbon sponsors founded Estoril and Monte Estoril on the right bank of Rio Tejo west of Lisboa. King Philip III traded from Madrid with his Viceroy as agent in the city.

Significantly and regrettably, as was the case with Arabs on their caravans delivering gold across the Sahara Desert to North Africa, there are no records of articles of value reciprocally delivered to West Africa by Prince Henry's navigators in their caravels in 1452 or by their successors thereafter. This aspect of the trade between North Africa and later Portugal and West Africa should be borne in mind as the story continues.

One hundred and fifty but two, years after Portugal minted the cruzados from the first cargo of gold delivered directly from Sub-Saharan Africa, Dom Domingos, Prince of Oeri, embarked on one of Philip III's ships for Lisboa. During that interval, the voyage to West Africa, Sâo Tomé, and beyond had evolved from an adventure to a business enterprise that included both the lucrative ivory trade of the Congo and the farming of its taxes as duly acknowledged by the Crown.

After more than three weeks on the high seas, it was a relief to see land that defined the banks of the magnificent Rio Tejo estuary. After a short trip upstream, Dom Domingos, Prince of Oeri, was received and welcomed by the Viceroy.

The Prince's arrival in Lisbon marks the last beginning of this story. Lisbon, however, was not his final destination. After careful consideration of Olu Sebastian's request, King Philip and his Viceroy determined that the Prince should proceed to Royal Coimbra (pronounced Kwimbra) for his education. He would study at the Hieronymite Institute for Secular and Religious Studies— Colégio de S Jeronimo. It was a stone's throw from the Royal Palace of Coimbra that was perched on a fortress hill overlooking the Rio Mondego on its right bank.

Dom Domingos was disappointed to learn that he would not be proceeding directly to Coimbra. Arrangements for his board and schooling were yet to be finalized. A number of other reasons caused more delay. No proposals or requests could be submitted to various authorities until he had presented himself in Lisboa. Negotiations with the bureaucracy of the Royal Treasury for funds to support him at the residential College could not be hurried. Additional difficulties arose from the fact that the approval of various decisions had to be obtained from the King, who was some distance away in Madrid. Delay was inevitable. The Prince was encouraged to use the waiting period to write letters to his father and read books from the Viceroy's library.

In 1601, however, the King informed the Viceroy that Dom Domingos, Prince of Oeri, was now expected at Colégio de S Jeronimo. He had been accepted for admission; the arrangements for the disbursement of an annual pension of 200,000 reis by the College Authorities had been approved. All who had been involved in the process of placing the Prince welcomed the announcement.

Personally, it gave the Prince considerable satisfaction and joy. Not only would he begin his studies at Coimbra, but he was granted a secret wish and desire held since he arrived in Lisboa. He would undertake his first journey on land in a novel structure that held several people secured on a platform with moving parts; it was drawn by a set of *elefante*—the largest animals he had ever seen!

The excitement of boarding was replaced by the striving to adjust to the swaying, tossing, and physical restrictions of the coach. The early discomfort was also soon forgotten as the changing landscape unfolded before them. From the wetlands of the riverbanks to the open fields of green flatlands and the undulating highlands that stretched westward in the distance, the kaleidoscope of images fascinated a youth whose appreciation of landscape had been limited to the beaches of riverine settlements! Admiring the scenery between stops at Vila Franca de Xira and Santarein to rest or change horses, eat, and perform necessary intimate personal functions occupied the first day of the journey and readied him for the night's layover at Entroncamento.

After an early breakfast the next day, the ride began in the southern basin of the amazing Rio Zezere with its myriad tributaries. They passed the City of Tomar then headed north to the highlands of Leira and Coimbra counties where the Prince spent the night at Penela. This arrangement made the next morning's crossing of the Mondego at Santa Clara the appropriate time to arrive at the Colégio de S Jeronimo for processing by the authorities.

The Colégio de S Jeronimo was the perfect student setting for Dom Domingos. With its residential facility run by Hieronymite priests, the Academy fostered intellectual development during his adolescent years that were spent away from home. Religion was, as would be expected, a significant aspect of life in the Colégio and the city even before the latter became the center of controversy in the ecclesiastical world in 1325. That year Queen Isabella petitioned Pope Clement V for permission to build the Monastery de Santa Clara on the left bank of the Mondego in the face of fierce opposition by the Cruzos, the highest religious order in Portugal.

The Prince took advantage of the scholastic opportunities offered to him in Coimbra and applied himself to his education. His ensuing academic success was soon demonstrated in a petition to King Philip in July 1604 in which he asked to proceed to Lisboa to study Latin and other good disciplines for three years, provided he was not recalled by his father. In a period of just over two years, he had achieved a level of education that indicated he would soon be qualified for admission into the highest institution of education in Portugal. Let there be no doubt about this conclusion. If the petition was improper in any way, neither the College's Faculty nor the Viceroy would have allowed it to be forwarded.

The King's immediate, enthusiastic granting of the petition was in itself remarkable. But even more remarkable were the orders or commands issued with the granting:

1. He was to be received in Lisbon by both the Rector of the Augustinian College and Viceroy who were to see that he was taken in, lodged suitably as befit his station, and treated with all proper courtesy;
2. The Prince's establishment was to be enlarged to include a tutor, to be appointed by the Rector of the college, and two servants;
3. To cover the extra expenses, the Prince's pension was to be increased as of January 1607 to 320,000 reis per annum and to be paid directly to the Rector who would supervise the Prince and control his expenses as well as his household staff.

As might be expected, over time, more than the essentials of the King's Orders became known, for better or for worse, in various circles of the Lisbon Society, which immediately and unavoidably made the Prince an instant Lisbon celebrity.

Ignatius Loyola, a Spanish soldier and clergyman, had founded the Roman Catholic Church Order of the Society of Jesus in 1534. It is not very surprising that a year later, in 1535, a Province of the Society was functioning in neighboring Portugal with the Provincial (who was the head of the Province or local district of the Society's chapter) resident in the populous City of Lisboa. Because of the Jesuits' interest or expertise in education, the Provincial was invested with authority to create a new institution that would supplement the University of Lisboa, which was founded in 1290. At the time of Dom Domingos's arrival in Portugal during the first decade of the seventeenth century, however, there were two uncompleted structures. These were the result of a strategy that for many years alternated the new university's location between Lisboa and Coimbra with both remaining firmly under the Provincial's control. Such was the higher education in the country.

In the March 1606 scholastic peregrinations, King Philip ordered the Rector of the Jesuit College of Santo Antão in Lisboa to receive Dom Domingos, Prince of Oeri, into the College. The Rector's initial flippant response was direct. In his considerable experience in the field, he had not known of a Negro with the Prince's level of education. He suggested that the Prince acknowledge and be satisfied with this achievement; further, it would be in the Prince's best interest to return to Africa. When it was apparent that the King would insist on his request, the Prince's admission to the College immediately developed into a battle. The Rector and the Provincial of the Jesuits argued against the King and his Viceroy. The Provincial informed the King that the Santa Antão College was not yet completed and therefore, or because of it, lodgings suitable for a Prince were not yet available. The King then asked that the Prince be admitted to the College at Coimbra. Since the Prince had been a student in Coimbra, he would continue in the same vein and require very little different in the way of accommodation.

The Provincial delayed his reply until September. Nothing was available in Coimbra either. The King was exasperated by the tactics and intention of the Jesuits; their rejection of the student Prince was not based on academic qualification, which was the basic criterion for admission. On October 31, the King decided that something had to be done. He ordered the Jesuit Rector of the Santo Antão College to hire lodgings for the Prince and his servants in Lisboa where his conduct, household, and expenses were to be supervised by the Rector as though he were living in the College. Not surprisingly, the Rector's choice was not very satisfactory because Dom Domingos complained of them in April 1607. The Viceroy agreed with the Prince and suggested that he be given an extra lodging allowance of 40,000 reis to enable the Rector to obtain a more suitable accommodation.

Dom Domingos in Portugal: In High Society

K ing Philip III of Spain and Portugal originally was involved only marginally in the affairs of Oeri. The Bishop of Sâo Tomé, Francisco de Vila Nova, asked him for help in setting up a Missionary Outpost in the Oeri Kingdom in the last decade of the sixteenth century. The King's response was both practical and revealing.

He agreed with the Bishop's suggestion that the trade in slaves should extend into Olu Sebastian's territory. This eventually brought the word Escravos into local use; but there was a provision in the authorization to exempt the Christian natives of Oeri Kingdom from the trade as their spiritual salvation should be the Bishop's prime consideration.

King Philip was a Christian King dealing in slaves, but Itsekiri Christians of the Oeri Kingdom were not to be sold into slavery. This concern most likely made it easy, or at least not a great leap, for him to accept responsibility for the education of an African-Christian Prince at the Bishop's request. This acceptance was a total commitment as evidenced upon the Prince's arrival in Portugal. From Dom Domingos's placement in the Colégio de St. Jeronimo in Royal Coimbra with a generous pension to the battle with the hierarchy of the Society of Jesus for the Prince's admission to Santo Antão College, the King's support was resolute. Most remarkable, however, were the commands associated with his accelerated grant of the Prince's petition to "study Latin and other good disciplines" even if it came after indisputable academic success in Coimbra.

It is to the King's credit (great if not eternal) to have reminded the Viceroy and the Rector of the Augustinian College of the Prince's station and that they must treat him with all proper courtesy. Throughout the history of Christendom, it will be difficult indeed to find any comparable recognition, acknowledgement, or acceptance of an African Royal. Unfortunately, the King's recognition of Dom Domingos as Royalty may have produced unexpected results. This included the refusal by the Provincial of the Jesuits and the Rector of Santo Antão College to admit the Prince into their institution.

Could he, who wore the regal diadem of Spain, have foreseen a battle fought with priests of an Order of the Church with Spanish beginnings over the education of a Christian African Prince that would last more than six months? Could he have foreseen that it would take place in Portugal away from the King's Court in Madrid? Not likely!

Whether this confrontation was an isolated response of institutional jealousy and bigotry or perhaps the tip of public resentment or discontent remained to be seen. It is an understatement to say that the individual who was at the heart of the Santo Antão College admission controversy was perplexed. Since childhood, he had known only kindness and courtesy from the priests of the Order of St. Augustine, and these considerations had been extended to him during his student days in Coimbra. As far as he was aware, there were no adverse reports from Coimbra that would have suggested or recommended excluding him from a college community; nor did he have previous contacts with members of the Society of Jesus that would lead to the justification of such shameless prejudice. The inflexibility of the Jesuits was bewildering. The Jesuit hierarchy exploited the King's genuine concern to ensure that an African Prince received basic courtesy demanded by protocol to advance their personal or institutional prejudice. There are no records of responses or reactions from the Prince, but the unsatisfactory lodgings provided, directly or indirectly, by the Rector were so outrageous that he was forced to file a complaint with the King for the first time during his seven years sojourn in Portugal.

The Prince of Warri studied Latin and the other good disciplines of his choice at the Santa Antão College after he was enrolled in 1606. However, he did not restrict himself to purely academic pursuits as the following Royal Decree demonstrates:

I, the King, make it known to those who shall see this my decree that, considering what great service to God and myself would follow the opening up of the ports, commerce, and trade of the Kingdom of Oeri on the Coast of Guinea, both in the establishment of divine worship and in the promulgation of our holy Catholic faith by bringing to true knowledge of it, the inhabitants of the said Kingdom and the infidels and idolaters of those parts; as also what profit and utility may result from this for my Kingdoms and dominions and for the inhabitants themselves of the said Kingdom, did order the Counselors of my Treasury to consider this matter and seek information from persons who live in and sail to these parts and accepting the recommendations of the said Council and the endeavors they have made in the case, I hold it good and it pleases me for all the said respects and because Dom Domingos, son of the King of Oeri in the name of said King has petitioned me to grant him that the said ports of his Kingdom, should be open to trade, with all my vassals of these Kingdoms and Dominions of Portugal; that in them, trade shall be conducted from now henceforth as and in the manner which it is conducted in the Kingdom of Congo and this Decree shall be fully observed as in the manner herein related without any doubt or hindrance whatsoever. (12.23.1607).

Aside from the light shed on King Philip's personal faith and desire for what was in his own best interest and that of Portugal's, the Royal Decree shed considerable light on both his high regard for the King of Oeri and his pride in Dom Domingos. It was also a statement of triumph for Dom Domingos in that it buttressed previous favorable Royal opinion of him and provided public commendation for his apparent self-application in extracurricular activities judged of benefit to the Kingdom of Oeri. And, in a personal way, it was a source of great pride and satisfaction to Father Manoel d' Almeida, Personal Chaplain to Dom Domingos. He and the Prince had emerged unscathed from the drawn-out admission controversy involving the Provincial and the Rector of Santo Antão College. The release of the Royal Decree on 12.23.1607 provided Dom Domingos and a widening circle of admirers and well-wishers a yuletide of more to celebrate than the birth of Jesus Christ. And thereby hangs a tale!

High Society

The Head of Household was at the door of the study when Dom Domingos reached for it after overhearing voices in conversation in the hallway "Father Manoel," he announced briefly before turning to go. It was 8:00 a.m. on December 24, 1607, and Dom Domingos wondered why his Personal Chaplain was at the residence so early. It did not take long before Father Manoel d'Almeida satisfied his curiosity.

After briefly exchanging greetings, Father Manoel said, "Dom Christovao has asked us to join his family for Christmas Dinner. Apparently, his attention was drawn to the Decree yesterday. Remembering our relationship, he sent a message to me indicating that he and his family would be happy to be our hosts on Christmas Day. I, of course, accepted his gracious invitation and came to inform you that it now supersedes our prior commitment. I have arranged for transportation to be here at noon tomorrow so that we arrive in good time before the meal."

"But Father…" Dom Domingos sputtered, trying to cut in without success.

"The setting," Father Manoel continued, "would provide an opportunity for congratulations on your successful work with the Decree as well as one for you to meet the rest of the family. Of course, I also hope it will be a very good and satisfying dinner."

"Yes, I know, Father. But…" stumbled Dom Domingos as his Personal Chaplain finished speaking.

"Pardon my hurried departure. I stopped by early to inform you so that I did not surprise you tomorrow."

"All right, Father," said the Prince, shrugging his shoulders in a realization that further discussion or argument would not be fruitful.

Father Manoel d'Almeida first met Dom Christovao Pereira as a young and newly ordained priest assigned to the Carmo Church of the Carmo Convent. Dom Christovao, as he was popularly known, faithfully tended the tomb of Imao Nuno de Santa Maria in the nave of the Church; placing flowers on it on feast days and generally ensuring it was well kept. After the Father read the inscription at the tomb head (refer to Appendix 1) he realized that Dom Christovao's full name was Dom Christovao Pereira. As the son of the fourth Earl and Lord of Santa Maria da Feira (Dom Diogo Pereira) brother of the then fifth Earl and Conde da Santa Maria Feira (Joao Pereira Forjaz), he had the same ancestry as the Friar interred at the Church.

Nuno Alvares Pereira, Constable to the first King John (father of Prince Henry the Navigator); grandson of the ninety-seventh Archbishop of Braga (Dom Alvaro Goncalves Pereira), and father of the first Duchess of Braganza (Beatrice Pereira de Alvin), forsook all to be a Friar at the Convent as Nuno de Santa Maria. The story of the evolution of friendship between the priest and a faithful keeper of the Pereira Legacy had been shared with Dom Domingos at some time before the Christmas of 1607.

It was obvious on their arrival that Father Manoel was a popular guest at the home of Dom Christovao Pereira. This was particularly evident among the younger generation, making it a particularly warm welcome for the Priest and the Prince. Before dinner, the host's noble family was extremely gracious to Dom Domingos. In addition to showering him with praise and congratulations on his work with the Decree, they also needled him in good humor about the publicized difficulties he had with the Provincial and the University Rector.

The dinner, which really was a banquet, more than met Father Manoel's expectations. The extravagant meal was followed by a musical presentation. The Pereira daughters then skillfully directed the young guests to a separate and self-contained area. They anticipated the conversation would be less restricted in scope or content and characterized more by the unpredictable reactions of the loud laughter or hush of youth!

Just when Dom Domingos became aware that he had continuously occupied a seat adjacent to one of the Pereira daughters and had been absorbed in rather earnest conversation with her during that period of time, Father Manoel's voice floated across the room. "Dusk is setting in; however reluctantly, we should be going home."

As Dom Domingos rose to express appreciation and gratitude to his hosts, he felt the firm clasp and squeeze of a small hand that made him turn to meet an unexpectedly warm smile with his own. Soon thereafter, he and his fellow guest completed their obligations to their hosts, Dom Christovao and his Lady, and boarded their carriage for their return journey home.

Days later, as Domingos and Father Manoel were leaving the Sunday-after-Christmas Mass, Dom Christovao hailed them. After exchanging greetings, Christovao thanked them for honoring his invitation to the family's Christmas dinner and informed them of the enthusiasm generated by their presence among family members.

"They all hope that it was not your final appearance during the Season," he said. In the spirit of fulfilling that anticipation, he invited them to stop for mid-morning refreshments if it was not inconvenient. Since Father Manoel and the Prince were expected for the mid-day meal at the Priory located in the vicinity, a brief stay at the Pereira's home was not particularly disruptive of their Sunday schedule. Therefore, they gladly accepted the invitation.

At the Pereira residence, family and guests were engaged in more than a renewal of acquaintances. Because everyone was in a festive mood, it seemed of no special significance that Maria and the Prince were immersed in conversation. At that first opportunity of meeting again after Christmas Day, she extended to him, as if on her father's behalf, her own personal invitation to the family's New Year's Day House Party.

A Fateful Party

The New Year's Eve party at the Periera's was already in progress when Dom Domingos arrived. Despite the apparent chaos of noise and movement created by children and adults everywhere, Maria was at the doorway to welcome him. He, at this third visit to the house, was familiar with the Periera family members and his surroundings.

He was soon engaged in conversation with his hosts and their guests. When supper was announced, Maria took him to a set table for a meal that would be every young man's wish for dinner. The Prince, however, tried to live up the advice "Everything in moderation."

After supper, the Prince and Maria were continually engrossed in their "own" almost private conversation until the lengthening of shadows could not be conveniently ignored. It was the signal for the Prince to take his leave. They walked a few yards from the mansion; then his hand found hers and they continued hand in hand towards his carriage. Just beyond a turn at the courtyard, they were inexplicably in an embrace that was unlocked only by the sound of her purse hitting the cobblestones and his effort to support her and prevent her from slipping from his arms. Mutterings of mutual apologies spluttered through their lips as they struggled to remain on their feet. It was rather, as may be imagined, disconcerting for both young adults. However, they instinctively recognized their emotional circumstance. While one became certain, the other was nonplussed and apprehensive.

At home that night, the Prince's unsettling encounter returned to haunt him. What if he, Prince of Oeri, Dom Domingos, has been observed in that act of embracing a foreign woman and then through various channels of communication the incident was reported to his father and from there to the Oeri people. "Dom Domingos was seen behaving shamefully in public and in broad daylight in Portugal," the Palace detractors will announce everywhere. "He is not, in truth, the student about whom all the Christian activities have been portrayed. He should not have been allowed to stray from home." These were the possible gossip lines that would be spreading in Oeri.

He had to, if possible, immediately forestall such an outcome or something worse ensuing from the encounter.

He woke early the next morning for confession with Father Manoel. Then he returned home to write a letter to his father advising him that his education was at a level that ensured a capability to successfully undertake all assignments in Oeri. As soon as his father's summons for his return home was in his hands, he would ask the Viceroy for release from college.

In early February, Dom Domingos informed the Viceroy, who was also the Inquisitor General, that he had received a summons from his father for his return home. Accordingly, he sought permission to travel to Madrid to take leave of the King. Advising against the return, the Viceroy suggested that the recall was a fabrication.

The Prince was ordered to continue his studies until he could produce a letter from his father confirming the summons. In his now disciplined way of life, as soon as he had determined that he should return home, Dom Domingos began work on a memorandum of personal, family, and State (Oeri Kingdom) requests that in essence was a follow-up to the Decree. It was submitted late that summer after he received the letter confirming the summons from his father. The King's reply was not received until February 1609.

Apart from the significance or relevance of its individual items, the document and annotated replies (refer to Appendix 2) illustrate various aspects of the Prince's mature thinking. It demonstrates his understanding of the fundamentals of a successful State. He wrote that the State's survival and ability to thrive depended on trade and its ability to defend both itself and that trade. Further in this vein, the request for personal armor was an acknowledgement of his Edo heritage and acceptance of the ancestral royal responsibility of personally leading the Kingdom in war. The King also instructed that the Prince be given 500 cruzados on his return from Santiago de Compestela.

The mention of the city of Santiago de Comestela in the King's reply provides an opportunity to revisit Olu Sebastian's letter to King Philip III requesting the Prince's education in Portugal. It asked that his son be instructed in European ways so that he might help his father in the conversion of his people and in the government of the kingdom.

The request provides a window into the expectations for the Prince's future life. His religious activities, which were limited at home in Oeri because of the nature of the existing facility, expanded considerably in his student days in Cambria. There were daily compulsory worships at the college chapel as well as Sunday Mass and catechism classes at the cathedral on Rao do Norte, a short distance from the college; but they were not the totality of his devotional duties. Added to these institutional commitments were participation in festivals and visits to churches and religious landmarks in the city.

After his first visit to the tomb of Queen Isabel of Aragon on the left bank of the Mondego River, he ordered his life in a new direction of active personal involvement in religion. Rainha Santa, the Saint Queen, also known as the Peacemaker, was sculptured in limestone. Her image was posed supine with hands clasped on her pilgrim's staff and a full purse of alms on display. Saint James, whose supposed worldly remains were at the pilgrim's destination of the Cathedral of Santiago de Compestela, looked on from a crypt in a scene that captured the Prince's imagination. The pilgrim who left all her gold at her destination became a Clarist nun at the monastery she built by license from Pope Clement V. Her tenacity and perseverance in the face of fierce opposition of the Cruzios—the Monks of Santa Cruz and the highest religious order of the land— impressed Dom Domingos. Queen Isabel became his royal role model and inspired him to register as a member of the Church and commit himself to a life that would be worthy of the Church's pilgrimage tutorials.

The Prince was therefore a committed and recognized member of the Church in Coimbra. It was the communication of this fact to the Viceroy on his transfer to Lisbon that resulted in the assignment of Father Manoel d'Almeida as the Prince's Personal Chaplain. This relationship introduced him to the life story of another religious legend, Friar Nuno de Santa Maria and eventually to Dom Christovao Pereira. The home of Dom Christovao was the site of the emotional New Year's Day Courtyard incident. The incident and the Prince's reaction to it have been described. Whether the incident developed into a personal or emotional guilt crisis, considering the Prince's preceding five or six years of devout living in Portugal, and led to the Viceroy's subsequent rejection of an undocumented summons shall remain in conjecture.

In the summer of 1608, a new secular Viceroy accepted Olu

Sebastian's letter confirming the summons of his son. The Council of Portugal agreed that the Prince was sufficiently educated and should be given leave to return to Oeri. He was excused from the journey to Madrid to take leave of the King. Maria was surprised and disconcerted at this news. She confided in her mother that she believed the Prince was ending his stay in Portugal because of the developing relationship between them. She contemplated on the propriety of raising the issue with him.

Any possibility of turmoil in the home of Dom Christovao Pereira precipitated by his daughter's predicament was, however, dramatically averted. The Pereira family received the sad news of the death of Dom Christovao's brother, D. Joao Pereira Forjaz, the Fifth Earl and Conde de Santa Mara da Feira. The family was plunged into mourning with all of its implied constraints as well as its accepted rituals for individual expressions of condolences that also provided opportunities for focused discussions.

By February 1609, many months into the Pereira family's mourning and the occasion of the receipt of the King's reply to Dom Domingos's memorandum, a stable if low-key relationship existed between the prince and Maria. But this was about to change. The Prince's remarks about his forthcoming Pilgrimage, including his expected rest nights at the Monastery of Santa Clara (which had been vacated by the nuns because of flooding from the Mondego and turned into a Pilgrim's resting stage) and the opportunities for revisiting Rainha Santa's tomb, illuminated another facet of his life that Maria found moving and revealing.

On her own, and spontaneously, she asked her parents if family members at the Santa Maria de Feira Castle would consider hosting the Prince on one leg of his journey. The answer was illuminating and an education on the austerities of a Church-sponsored Pilgrimage Program. These pilgrimages were assigned designated shelters with documented times of arrival and departure for each member of the Church's group of pilgrims. Attendance at required

Masses and at stipulated locations were witnessed. Maria realized that the journey was not intended to be an excursion.

As the date of the Prince's departure approached, she now held a greater understanding and appreciation of what a pilgrim's daily life entailed. She increasingly reflected on his apparent unmindfulness of the hardships that contrasted with the joyfulness at the prospect of reaching a religious destination at Santiago de Compostela. Her reflection, initiated in worry, became dominated by anxiety and wonder.

His absence brought no relief from her emotional quandary. At Church, she sought out Father Manoel after Mass to enquire if he had news of his especial parishioner. At home, she only pecked at the food on her plate and delayed bedtimes for no obvious reason. As these behaviors became more frequent and difficult to ignore, things came to a head one evening.

"Yes, he's gone far beyond familiar Santarem and Entroncamento," Maria murmured aloud. "He surely must have been at home in Coimbra and Santa Clara, but what about Santa Maria da Feira, Porto, or Braga? How did he...,"— she murmured as her bedroom door opened. "Oh goodness, I am sorry that I disturbed you, Mother. I did not realize that...I will go to sleep now." But that was not easy to accomplish. A book had opened involuntarily in her mind, and she read it silently. "The Provincial of the Jesuits, the Rector of the Jesuit College, and, in days to come, Francisco Cavarlho, Judge of the Court of Appeals and His Household Staff, looked at him and saw the Beast and were blinded beyond that by prejudice, bigotry, or resentment."

Maria, looked through that same color of his skin and saw a complex, cultivated, yet considerate, person. Here was a foreigner who spoke the Portuguese language in all its nuances as well as Latin and that native tongue of his too! One who could talk with a King (the Decree), and not lose the common touch (Requests for his Household Staff in the Memorandum). He was a Prince and so remained as he held his own counsel while the admission controversy raged openly. He did not wear his religion on his sleeve but was faithfully retracing his Royal Heroine's (the Peace Maker's) footsteps to pay homage to Saint James the Apostle at Santiago de Compestela in remote Northwestern Spain. But he also wanted a personal steel armor to wear in battle. All of these were true enough for her. Did only she see this?

The sunlight that pierced through the window from the late morning's blue sky woke her. She had, after all, fallen into a long restful sleep. Although she felt sprightly, a calm had settled inside her—the worry and anxiety, or even wonder, was resolved.

She recognized what it was that brought her mother to her door last night. She was yearning for his return and that yearning was greater than desire. Her love was not blind. No. Not one little bit! It was discerning and admiring. More importantly, her love was caring, very caring. Her "book" had revealed the one with whom she wanted to spend the rest of her life; if only that unique person....

After Mass on Sunday, she saw Father Manoel at some distance from the family group. He nodded his head excitedly in a direction as if asking her to meet him separately. "Yes, I heard from my special parishioner! He paid homage to Saint James and hopes to attend Mass here next Sunday. Oh! He sends his greetings to you and, through you, to the family." Father Manoel proclaimed to her with a broad smile.

"Thank you," she said. "It is kind of you to deliver his message. I will relay his greetings to the family."

Dom Christovao almost cheered when the family was informed of the Prince's successful pilgrimage and his greetings. "This deserves a celebration," he said. "A successful pilgrimage," he paused as he made the sign of the Cross on his head and chest, "should be commemorated by family. However, since Dom Domingos's only family appears to be Father Manoel, who I am certain will be making arrangements for that occasion in his honor, as I speak." He turned and asked his wife, "Will you, my dear, consider helping him out here at the house?"

"Of course," she replied almost before the end of the question. "But we need a volunteer to inform Father Manoel of our proposal as soon as possible," and looked at Maria with a telling, yet tender, smile.

Dom Christovao Pereira and his wife had concluded as witnesses to Maria's recent behavior that she was a Pereira. Their daughter's developing and openly acknowledged relationship with an African Prince reminded them of the Pereira's individualism of past eras: a married Archbishop Pereira and father of nineteen children; a boy soldier, Nuno Pereira, whose initial singular nobility support of King John in the battles of the Castile War of Independence from Spain was crucial to the King's success. Maria displayed the independence of mind that was very likely to not only accommodate the thought but also the consummation of a marriage outside the conventional. She probably would follow her heart. It was desirable, indeed preferable, if not best for them to provide Maria an environment that allowed her to reach a fully considered decision without intrusion or apparent coercion—especially as they inadvertently had provided an opportune moment.

If the period of time in which a life is transformed or reshaped can later be seen as only an instant, this was Maria's moment. The soliloquy generated by personal turmoil followed by the opening of a door, good news, and parental embracement with tacit and almost palpable encouragement, telescoped into an experience of inner joy from which a new frame of mind emerged. Maria quietly accepted her mother's challenge and publicly acknowledged her life's direction.

As soon as Dom Domingos arrived back n Lisbon, Father Manoel confirmed the arrangements for the Prince's special thanksgiving offering for the accomplishment of his cherished ambition of pilgrimage to Santiago de Compestela. At the 10:00 am mass the next Sunday, one of the officiating priests announced approval of a special offering for the Prince of Oeri, Dom Domingos, after the celebration of the feast of communion. At the appointed time, Father Manoel led the Prince the foot of the altar. Turning to the congregation he related Domingos's successful pilgrimage to Santiago de Compestela and proffered a prayer of thanksgiving. The simple brief narrative was impressive enough to evoke congratulations and a blessing.

Before lunch at the Pereira's home, which had become a familiar destination for the Prince and his Personal Chaplain, moments and situations succeeded one another until, as if prearranged, he and Maria were together by themselves.

He did ask her! On this occasion, with hands free and her feet firmly planted on the ground, she looked into his eyes. The unspoken question, "Why did it take you so long?" was written all over her face. But she simply said, "Yes!" and embraced him tightly.

When emotions had ebbed to even and customary levels, he broke the silence. "Father Manuel says he'll be honored to look after everything ecclesiastical."

"Really?" she asked straightening herself up to her full height. But she was already in a mood that would let certain indiscretions go unchallenged or unacknowledged. She simply smiled.

The wedding was a private affair; its existence was not introduced into the public consciousness until two months later in June 1609. By this time, his household staff had increased significantly to cater for him and his newly wedded wife. There was, however, growing resentment in certain quarters of his obviously upgraded standard of living and lifestyle. It surfaced as a brawl between servants of the Prince and the neighboring household of Francisco Carvalho, a Judge of the Court of Appeals, and the latter's response. Carvalho was so angered by the behavior of the Prince's servants that he sent the official and several men to Domingos's residence one night to arrest the servants. They did so after breaking down the doors with great noise as if it were a murder. When Domingos complained, the King asked the Viceroy to look into the matter and that full satisfaction be given to the Prince. For reasons that were only obvious to him, however, the Viceroy laid the blame for the incident at Domingos's feet.

In August, the Prince received a command, from the King, to leave the country with the shortest possible delay. For some, this command indicated a frosty relationship in place of a previously and publicly recognized cordiality. The Prince wrote to the King giving the reasons for his continued stay and set out certain unfulfilled commitments that begged the King's consideration.

Less than thirty days later, on September 22, 1609 the King ordered the Viceroy to investigate the points raised and report to him so that the Prince might sail for Africa as soon as possible.

Soon thereafter, Dom Domingos and his wife sailed for Warri/ Oeri City in a ship of the Royal fleet bound for São Tomé. He was provided with a complete set of steel armor and weapons and was accompanied by ten servants, four of whom were earlier knighted, at his request, by the King.

The voyage from Lisbon to Oeri City in the Royal Ship proved to be routine and lasted about thirty days. No dangers or situations calling for help or assistance at any of the Portuguese forts or ports on the West Coast of Africa were encountered. Eleven years after the Prince left home to study in Portugal, Olu Atoneongboye (Olu Sebastian) welcomed Dom Domingos and his Portuguese wife with great joy and religious festivities. In the same manner that his father, Olu Esigie, had quickly transferred the responsibility for making the Kingdom function as a successful enterprise upon his return from São Tomé, Olu Sebastian soon informed Domingos that the future of the Kingdom was now in his hands.

The Prince did not succeed his father until 1625, fifteen years after he and his wife arrived in Oeri. During those years and thereafter, he visibly changed the character and fortunes of the Kingdom. The Trade Mission, which as a student in Lisboa he had implored King Phillip to establish, was created. He also expanded commerce with trade in peppers and spices.

Oeri City became a well recognized and cherished outpost of Christendom with a resident priest, clergymen, and visiting Bishops who utilized the facilities first erected by Olu Sebastian and then modified and expanded by Dom Domingos.

This religious aspect of life in Oeri was of great importance to the Prince who was a dedicated Christian working with his father to "bring the citizens of the Kingdom into the Church."

The success of the Christian work in the field was mirrored in his personal life. His marriage proved to be a successful union that raised three sons—all of whom were educated in Portuguese institutions in Angola. His devotion to his Portuguese wife was apparent as he never remarried after her death.

António Domingos Omonigheren: Prince with Golden Skin

By all accounts, Dom Domingos's sojourn and education in Portugal were put to good services on his return home. He was able to promote the interests of the Kingdom, both spiritually and commercially, and make Oeri relevant to interests of Europe's trading and exploring power during the first half of the seventeenth century. Indeed, according to some, "Dom Domingos must be credited the flourishing of the Portuguese Missions (Christianity and Trade) in Warri during the first half of the seventeenth century."

It is also relevant and significant that during his student days in Portugal and after his return to Oeri there is no record of discussions or proposals of his involvement with the Slave Trade. This is, however, not surprising. King Philip had indicated to the Bishop of São Tomé, "The spiritual salvation of the people of Warri should be of prime consideration."

The heir and successor to Dom Domingos, who, had he lived in Portugal would have been known as António Domingos Pereira, was a compelling personality on his own merit. In his youth, he was popularly known as Omonighenren, (Prince with the golden skin). As Olu Oyenakpagha, he was also known as, Obanigheren, King with the golden skin.

After his father, who brought the Robes of the Order of Christ,

71

a Crown, and other regalia from Portugal as a Prince, he was the second Olu crowned as a Christian King in Itsekiriland. Very personable, he wore Portuguese attire with a sword on his side. He had been well educated informally at home and at an Institute in Angola. He would use his knowledge of the Portuguese language to his advantage during his reign.

At his coronation, he struck a deal with the Church. He asserted that his father had remained a Christian and a monogamist only because he was married to a Portuguese lady. He would remain a Christian and eschew polygamy, the status favored by the priests, only if the Church sought a Portuguese lady to be his Queen. Unwilling to lose the only Christian King in West Africa, the Church complied by bringing a lady from Sâo Tomé who was joyfully received on arrival and raised a family for him.

He used his expertise of the Portuguese language to his advantage and the benefit of the Kingdom throughout his reign as is illustrated in his letter to Pope Clement X (refer to Appendix 2). That the letter, written in 1652, was successfully delivered at the Vatican is an achievement that reveals a considerable talent to devise and contrive what might be considered in the framework of his times a daunting undertaking. That it was retained in the Vatican Archives for three centuries (and it is believed remains there) before it was released for translation from Portuguese into English speaks to its unique nature in the context of the history of the Roman Catholic Church in West Africa in particular and in Africa generally. It is also a document that (without exaggeration) is remarkable as a study in the art of communication and supplication.

But more than the Prince's skill with words and his mastery of the art of supplication are evident in the letter. His Christian Faith, his work for and vision for the future of the Church, which he incidentally inherited, as well as his relationship with his parents and unnamed Portuguese "benefactors" are laid bare therein before his Holiness.

Pope Clement X must have been singularly impressed as he granted António Domingos's request in totality by ordering the return of the Capuchin Priests to Oeri City.

Equally remarkable is that his cousin, King John IV of Portugal (the Eighth Duke of Braganza when he ascended to the throne of Portugal as the first King in the line of the Fourth Dynasty in 1640), provided the "funds for the priests' passage and the necessary provisions."

António Domingos (also Obanighenren) was an optimist. In retrospect, he may have been too much of one. In his letter to Pope Clement X, he stated, "I will give them (referring to the Capuchin Fathers) all the help in my power and reliable interpreters so that they may bring my neighbor, the King of Benin, and others to the faith." His wish was not fulfilled at the time of his death in 1654, barely two years after he wrote the letter. Suffice it to say that the prize to convert the King of Benin to Christianity as of the twenty-first century remains out of reach.

But how could Omonighenren, the prince with golden skin be the person he came to be in the absence of that distinctive Iginua inherent or inherited disposition? When Prince Iginua was, in effect, summarily expelled from the Edo Kingdom and Empire to the wetlands of the riverines, he did not have much more than optimism and, in contrast to his Edo palace peers, the willingness to embrace the new, the different, or the foreign. To some extent, he and each of the successor Princes survived the threats of forced return, sudden deaths, and ubiquitous mosquitoes as well as separations, reunions, and the uncertainties of foreign relations to continuously expand the boundaries of that attitude to create a new way of life that was eventually and visibly expressed in the being of the colorful Omo-nighenren António Domingos.

For more than one hundred and fifty years, this attitude defined the Kingdom. It also sustained the group of individuals who comprised the Early Warri Princes and personified the Beginnings of a West African Dynasty that existed with uninterrupted continuity for two more centuries before its first interregnum in 1848.

Postscript

O n February 9, 2009, four hundred years to the month after Dom Domingos received the reply to his memorandum of requests to King Philip, I arrived in Portugal in attempt to visualize Prince Domingos's environment, if not his circumstance in the country. We may recall that the requests included the assignment of priests to Oeri, personal armor for himself and weapons for the state of Oeri. He also asked that a religious order be confirmed on him as well as some members of the family and increase in the amount of his personal allowance. The provision of a passage in one of King Philip's royal ships home to Oeri completed what may be described as the prince's wish list. The flight from London to Lisbon required flying high above a layer of dense clouds that were part of a weather system affecting most of Western Europe. It was only during the aircraft's final descent to Lisbon Airport that an occasional break in the clouds appeared. Even then, the rest of the day was uncommonly, for Portugal, grey and overcast.

I registered at my Estoril hotel and walked to the town's commercial center. After enquiring about the best way to reach the Lisboa terminal for the train journey to Coimbra, I went from the commuter train station through a tunnel to the shoreline of the Rio Teju. All the action on the river was from the wind and waves crashing on the beach and against abandoned piers. There was no marine traffic of significance as Lisbon's maritime trade was now carried out at Cascai. This busy port lay far west of the Tower of Belem that was built almost three centuries ago to guard the entrance to the City Port. The rest of my evening was spent on the boardwalk among mostly lightly clad jogging health enthusiasts!

The sun shone brightly the next morning as I stood with my new English speaking friend in a bus queue. Earlier, he had volunteered to assist me when he overheard my plea for help to getting to Coimbra at a food stall just outside Cais do Sodre, the busy commuter train station in Lisbon. After obtaining a ticket at a booth, we waited at the bus stop for the better part of half an hour.

When the specified bus arrived, he introduced me to the operator who "delivered" me to Santa Apolonia, Lisbon's railway terminal, about ten minutes later. At the ticket window, I was ever so nicely informed that I had missed a train for Coimbra by no more than a few minutes. Fortunately, another train was due in approximately thirty minutes. To purchase a ticket for that train journey, the clerk asked to see my passport. I produced and it without any visible or apparent phobia about cheating the nation. I was informed in a routine matter of fact manner, that I was eligible for a senior's discount on the fare. On my way to the waiting room, I wondered as I reflected on my good fortune so early in the day and thought: *Who is not my brother's keeper?*

It was a relief to read an unambiguous and familiar sign on Avenda Enidio Navarro in the city. After the challenges of Coimbra B, numerous station platforms, the sheltered terminal of a railroad spur and its shuttle cars for Coimbra A, and finally to arriving at "A." I entered the Hotel Astoria, registered without delay, and returned outside to start exploring my ultimate destination in Portugal where Dom Domingos, Prince of Oeiri, had been a student from 1601 to 1607.

In some ways, the Coimbra that reaches back to Arab and Roman occupation remains unchanged with spectacular views of and from the hill. Some major landmarks have new names and functions which only reflect the march of time.

Particularly helpful in my quest for information, however, was the Central Region Tourism Office located about one hundred meters from the hotel just beyond the *Largo* (plaza) at the foot of the Ponte de Santa Clara. Asked to return the next day for the answer to my question regarding the Hieronymite College that was in the city in the first decade of the seventeenth century, I duly presented myself at the appointed time of 1 p.m., after a bus tour of the Old City that included the University and the Old Cathedral.

The Institution was Colégio de S Jeronimo, which retained its independent status until 1834 when it was stripped of its monastery and convent to become part of the University of Coimbra. In 1836, once the students were transferred to the university campus, the facility was transformed into a Children's Hospital. When the latter found a new home, the buildings were demolished. No standing structure or building of Colégio de S Jeronimo remains in the twenty-first century.

So also, ironically, was that body of men known as the Society of Jesuits of the Province of Portugal. After wresting control from the local authorities and keeping a firm grip on the University of Coimbra for centuries (with its own Cathedral nearby), it was permanently barred from the country by the Republicans. The university was nationalized and shows no adverse effects from the change.

I was grateful for both the substance and duration of my discussions at the Tourism Office. I went out to the adjacent Riverside Park for refreshment and one final opportunity to view the scenery. The modernistic Ponte Raihna Santa Isabel was ahead of me; the Rio Mondego flowed silently on the right. With a half-turn to the left, I could see the sunlit University Hill with its tower and King John's Library.

It was not surprising that after a while of this restful interval, I realized the muttering of *milho* with the ho as in ho-ho. The word had been relegated to the subconscious in the hustle of travel after I promised to look into its pronunciation when I found it in a Brazilian-Portuguese/English dictionary. The rapport, ostensibly established in the previous hour or so, provided a good opportunity to ask, "Is it *milho* or is it *miyo*?"

Back to the Tourism Office; but my erstwhile instructor was not available. The young, African lady at the desk, however, was excellent. Indeed the ho-word was pronounced yo (as in yo-yo) almost the same as (I) miyo in Itskeri; and it did mean corn! A minor enlightenment, perhaps, but one so rewarding, it ensured the perfect end of my visit to Coimbra.

Light-footed and with a smile, I returned to the Hotel Astoria for my luggage and then on to "A" for my ticket to board the shuttle for "B" and the return journey to Lisboa.

In the next two days, there was not much I would see or experience that related to Dom Domingos's Lisboa, which had become Lisbon of the twenty-first century. The one continuous disaster of earthquake, fire, and tsunami that devastated the city in the eighteenth century did not spare many of its ancient landmarks, including Friar Nuno de Santa Maria's Church. There was, however, a new and striking landmark of sculptured men that demanded my attention each time the commuter train went by it. Though fascinating, and in some way compelling, I was neither able to admire it at close range nor singularly determine its significance before leaving Portugal.

This unsettling reaction to a monument, strangely, only began to be resolved during the last half hour of a previously planned three-day stopover in London. A late Friday night arrival and near midnight registration at the hotel was followed on Saturday morning by a futile attempt to redeem prescribed medications, unwittingly left at a Heathrow Airport Security checkpoint that Monday. On return to the city, sorefooted and tired, there was just sufficient time to make a Valentine's Day greeting call to the United States; a short respite reading my favorite United Kingdom newspapers— the *Guardian* and the *Independent*—before dinner, darkness, and bedtime in anticipation of a busy Sunday. The *Independent* was running a fourteen-day series of booklets titled *The World: A Pocket History*. That day, Part 8: "The classical world," appeared. Although I was tired, I read some of it and thought it of sufficient interest to retain it.

Next day, Sunday, two nieces I had promised to contact were sufficiently receptive to my pleadings of disability to come with their children for a prolonged and active visit in the hotel lobby. I particularly wanted to visit with one of them who since our last meeting had volunteered to come to the United States and help her sister who had suffered a stroke from a puerperal paradoxical embolus.

The appointment for time to be spent with Captain Robert Hayes, which would have been the second in eight days, was rescheduled to the following day due to traffic disruptions arising from maintenance work in the Underground system. But more about Captain Hayes later.

I won up early on Tuesday, February 17, for the journey to the airport. After completion of the various routine processes before boarding, I bought my newspapers for in-flight reading and sat down for a brief rest. The *Independent* booklet heading for that day was *The World: A Pocket History* Part 11: "Mediaeval Misery" was striking and arresting if not very promising. As I turned its pages to the "The Triumph of Death," "The Sack of Rome," "Attila the Hun," "English peasants' leader Wat Tyler meets his fate," "The Effects of the Black Death," and other calamities of Europe in mediaeval times. I remember wondering if it was worth reading. I was stunned when I reached page 18 (the last page). The statue honoring Prince Henry and his pioneering navigators looked me straight in the eye.

The call to board the aircraft for the flight to Newark was now competing for a response with the startling, mocking, but no less clear, "Do you remember me?" originating from the familiar and now captioned "Statue honoring Prince Henry and His pioneering Navigators, Lisbon." I got out my boarding pass, put the booklet in the carry-on, and proceeded to the gate. I had reading to do, starting with *The Great Escape: How an inquisitive Portuguese Prince initiated the Age of Discovery* the heading of the adjacent section.

I could now neither dismiss nor deny the possibility that the statue was in some way related to the purpose of my visit to Portugal and specifically to Lisbon. But how and why?

Fortunately, the internet provided answers to the question. The boy soldier who was one of the first noblemen to publicly support John of Avim's claim to the throne of Portugal, became King John's Second Constable and Lord Chamberlain. He was responsible for the stable environment that enabled Prince Henry to conduct his missions. Through his daughter's marriage, he became the founder of the House of Braganza and the Fourth Dynasty of Portugal. The life story of Nuno Pereira (alias Friar Nuno de Santa Maria) and its ramifications made the words of Olu Oyenakpagha of Warri (António Domingos Pereira) in his letter to Pope Clement X in 1652 vis-à-vis, "I am writing to my cousin King John of Portugal," reasonable and credible.

This reconstruction and determination from the results of the search, activated by the Lisbon statue as well as other findings and observations, made the visit to Portugal and the last leg of my odyssey a worthwhile endeavor.

My odyssey began many years ago when I questioned my inherent identity after a remark at a house party in the outreaches of suburban Red Hills in Kingston, Jamaica. I then reached out to my late friend Engineer Dediare in Nigeria and asked if he could arrange for me to visit various Itsekiri settlements during an upcoming leave of absence. It was, at that time, a different undertaking and experience to traverse the waterways of the Warri

Division of Delta State in unarmed canoes fitted with outboard engines compared with the situation that developed in the last decade of the twentieth century.

After visiting Orugbo, Ode Itsekiri, Usele, and Koko, I boarded a Nigeria Airways flight to London for my return journey to Jamaica. As the aircraft taxied under what could only be described as expert and confident hands to take off, I realized why my retort to certain disparaging remarks in Kingston was appropriate. I remained in my own world, almost in a trance, as we sped down the runway and then, effortlessly, breaking through a layer of clouds, soared into the sky.

When the aircraft reached cruising altitude, I felt a gentle nudge and turned to see Captain Hayes sitting beside me. As we exchanged greetings and pleasantries and recalled memories, it became apparent that he was conducting one of his training duties that, in turn, brought an understanding to a remarkable previous incident.

It occurred on a late afternoon when the first Nigeria Airways Aircraft, bringing General Gowon to the Kingston Jamaica Commonwealth Prime Ministers' Conference, made a perfect landing and taxied to a stop at the Norman Manley International Airport. When Captain Hayes and the first all non-Caucasian and African crew of an intercontinental jet aircraft flight emerged to form the receiving honor line for the General, they were met with unending jubilation and an almost riotous uproar in the public gallery. The crowd had come to acknowledge that the Nigerian crew had flown the aircraft more than 6,000 miles from Lagos Nigeria, West Africa, to Kingston, Jamaica. That was then!

Self-discovery, however, seemed to lose urgency after its first project was successfully completed with the Nigeria Airways flight from Ikeja, Lagos. Life's dislocations and relocations combined with their attendant decisions and consequences in many ensuing years demanded new priorities that were removed from the objectives of such a singularly oriented endeavor.

It was a sense of release from such obligatory responses, however, that one day generated an impulse to scribble *Beginnings of a West African Dynasty, A Saga of the Early Warri Princes*—a scribble as can be surmised now, modified on more than one occasion. All was not lost; the pursuit of the product of that impulse led to the reestablishment of a personal contact with Captain Hayes some thirty years after the Ikeja experience and less than one calendar year before traveling to Lisboa and Coimbra when a person on the telephone line of an unknown name, unknown number was identified!

But before that, I had received an invitation to attend a wedding in Benin City; yes, the Ubini of our story and the location of Oba Olua's palace and the origin of the Warri Princes. Despite these historical associations that might be perceived as significant, if not paramount considerations, the compelling reasons for accepting were the prospects of fellowship and renewal of acquaintances the occasion promised. No sooner had I reached the decision than a previous travel commitment came to mind— to visit Paul Bamela Engo, former Minister Plenipotentiary and Cameroun Ambassador to the United Nations, then judge, the International Court of the Law of the Seas, Hamburg, Germany, at his home in the Cameroun Republic that neighbors Nigeria. This reminder did not surface entirely on its own. Its trailer proposed a break during the stay in Yaounde for a visit to Sâo Tomé.

The rush to procure travel documents, confirm attendance of the wedding, as well as contact the Ambassador and obtain antimalarial drugs began soon thereafter. Fortunately, each objective was readily achieved. The entire exercise was capped by an enthusiastic response to a proposed Cameroun visit; it looked like a good African summer.

The wedding was, of course, special for the bride and groom. The anticipated reunion, too, did not disappoint—especially when some time after I had paid my respects to a very senior guest, he turned to one of his contemporaries and openly asked him to identify me, since he really did not recognize me. Since he had not seen me since I was in lower elementary or infant school and his (and his brother's) admission to King's College Lagos, the elite Nigerian Secondary School, was the talk of Warri, he could not identify me. That, however, proved not to be the only occasion on which I was, as it were, incognito in Benin City.

Chief Harriman, my host in Nigeria, had been granted an audience at the Palace on the Monday after the wedding. As a fellow Cambridge University graduate, local Oxbridge Club member, and colleague in other favorable connections, the Chief was in fairly regular contact with Oba Erediauwa. So his springing an audience at such short notice (I believed) was not, for him, extraordinary.

At the Palace Square, we were greeted by the Chief Vettor/Triage Officer. As far as he was concerned, I had my origins in Mars. However, since I was there with someone well known at the Palace, I would be allowed in. This brought us to a waiting chamber before admission to the Oba's presence. There, during the audience, I remained an enigma even though the Oba and the chief vettor were my (Order) House and School Prefects at Government College Ibadan and Ijebu Bypass Era. I last met with the Oba at the University of Benin when Professor Grace Alele-Williams, first Lady Head of a University in Africa, was Vice Chancellor.

We all appreciate the saying out of sight, out of mind; but after a while it all seemed bizarre. Could a supposed transformation in appearance be so complete that despite well-defined shared experiences, a remembrance or a recognition by one party was impossible? Perhaps. Happily, whoever I was on that day, if even as a solace, cherished gifts of Edo Bronze are reminders of a palace audience.

It was different in the Cameroun Republic on that Thursday, July 5, welcomed by Ambassador Engo at the Douala Airport and at the Yaounde luncheon party at Professor Victor Ngu's residence that brought back memories of Sundays past— Sundays of the first half of twentieth century Ibadan. First, though, we went westward from Douala with the Ambassador to recently flooded Limbe and the Southwest Seaboard resort area with its mountain-blue, majestic, and close, but never intimidating, shoreline accommodations and playgrounds dotted by volcanic rocks and enchanting offshore island hilltop homes with their seemingly, ever beckoning, evening lights. The region's renowned weather could not detract from the exhilarating scenic interplay of nature and man that fed the senses day and night during our sojourn. But soon, it was time to leave for Yaounde, the nation's capital, Cameroun's own capital city on seven hills. We traveled east through virgin African forestlands with picturesque waterfalls, lakes, and waterways.

Every nation's capital city has its parade grounds, monuments, and aspiring–to-be monumental, residential, legislative, administrative, and other structures. Obligatorily or otherwise, we visited all of these in Yaounde. Still, we sensed that these were only part of the experience the ambassador wanted to share. It was, therefore, no surprise that after a few days, we headed south to the Ambassador's hometown of Ebolowa for an elaborate and heartwarming welcome of entertainment, feasts, and gifts that occupied the better part of the weekend. Our experience continued as we traveled to Kribi, Cameroun's easternmost seashore resort. From the head of the escarpment, one can witness extraordinary sunsets at the ocean's horizon.

As we made our way back "home," I pondered my host's generosity, his family's embrace, and the spontaneous, untiring efforts to expose me to Cameroun's share of Africa's varied, fascinating, and unspoiled terrain. I also came to realize that in nearly two weeks of gracious hospitality, I had been unable to even mention my intended visit to São Tomé.

And when I did, I sensed a disappointment in the reply, "Since the arrangements for our visit to the Northwestern Province have not really been completed, this would be a good time for you to go." To my relief, and gratefulness, I procured the ticket to Sâo Tomé a day after our return to Yaounde.

At daybreak on July 19, we were on our way to Douala for my Air Cameroun flight to Libreville. From there, in the early afternoon, I was one of the ten passengers on a propeller aircraft flying west over the Atlantic Ocean to Sâo Tomé. On landing, I was informed that I needed an entry visa. The situation appeared ominous until I inquired where I could get an entry visa. "Here," the Immigration Officer indicated. In less than an hour after my small plane touched down, I had registered at the hotel and was admiring the scene on the Atlantic Sealane to the island from the marina.

It was disappointing but not, so far, frustrating. After five days, which included all of one weekend, I was familiar with the various precincts of the city but had little to show for information on sixteenth or seventeenth century Sâo Tomé. Not in desperation, but rather on the spur of the moment, as I walked by the Embassy of the Republic of Portugal, I entered the premises and asked if I could be given the opportunity for an interview with an English-speaking diplomat. After a short wait, I was ushered into an office and a surprisingly friendly atmosphere where I mentioned sixteenth century Sâo Tomé. I was politely informed that there was no one on the island who could help me at the Embassy and that there were no records relevant to my quest on the island. However, if I wished, I could be put in touch with someone who was visiting from Portugal.

It was not until my penultimate evening's social at the hotel that my contact appeared. He readily confirmed the situation regarding the island's records. He and his local companion considered my idea of visiting Angola to be ill -advised. He went on to provide a short list of historical texts, including Charles Boxer's *The Portuguese Seaborne Empire*, which he thought might be helpful.

My knowledgeable contact was a research fellow in linguistics on a summer project involving the Portuguese language and its interaction with (local) dialects of mainland African language. He seemed disappointed to hear of the rather imminent date of my departure. However, he appeared buoyed up at my reply, "I have not gone beyond the village south of the hotel."

He introduced me to "Teacher," the elementary school teacher of the city and the owner of a well-used Jeep. "Teacher would take us on a day trip tomorrow in his Jeep" was the next inevitable proposal. I eyed the means of transportation, but with really nothing to do the following day, I thought, *Why not*? We very quickly agreed upon a deal!

Next morning, the three of us, dissimilar persons, boarded Teacher's Jeep and headed south from the hotel. The excursion on the last full day of my visit was a jaunty expedition into the island's heartland with its mountains, waterfalls, forests, and the rivers that run in the rather narrow coastlands before emptying into the Atlantic Ocean.

In the quiet of its aftermath, as I waited for Teacher's transport to the airport, a perspective intruded into my consciousness and that first effort of self-discovery crystalized: today's journey, with its disappointing or enhancing moments, even in the absence of exciting and relevant paper trails, had its own merits as it expanded and colored the original, if sometimes mundane, search for yesterday. To wit, Sâo Tomé was not an imaginary or distant island in history. Indeed, it is a well traveled and fascinating present-day destination where once, more than four centuries ago, a Warri student Prince came ashore.

Spontaneously, that horizon and frame of mind was conjured up many years later in the journey through Portugal and brings us full circle to the beginning of this note to our story. The booklet, *The World: A Pocket History* obtained at the end of that journey, however, presented two new frames of mind for consideration. For centuries, the world has regarded the exploitation of the animal, vegetable, and mineral wealth of Africa and its peoples for the benefit of the rest of the world as a legitimate endeavor with barely token compensation or acknowledgement. As this does not directly touch our story, it shall not be further pursued.

The other related, personal, and intriguing consideration is that of a young lady of Portugal's Pereira ancestry. Late in 1609, she married Dom Domingos, Prince of Warri, on his return from Pilgrimage to Santiago de Compestela in northwestern Spain. She followed her heart and sailed with her husband from Lisbon to Warri in one of King Philip's merchant vessels.

No one has identified her frame of mind or the nature of her dowry as she undertook her voyage. She gave of herself to Africa. It is fair to assume from her son's letter to Pope Pius X that in that first half of the seventeenth century she was neither deserted nor abandoned. She and her husband continued the tradition of foreign education in the Ginuwa Dynasty, which, under the changed circumstances of the aforementioned interregnum and the advent of the British to the West Coast of Africa, underscores their success as well as her descendants' achievements outside of the Monarchy in the nineteenth and twentieth centuries. Through generations of ministers of religion and nuns, educators who included a university president or vice chancellor; professionals in the fields of law, medicine, and engineering; career military officers (admiral and general), and leaders in commerce, she is assured that any suggestion of sacrifice on her part would be summarily dismissed and indeed laughable.

At its end, this literary adventure is dedicated to the memory of a young lady who, four hundred years this autumn, sailed into a new life with her husband in a King's ship and two others, my mother and my daughter, who lived because of, and after, her as:

Mary Lilias aka Ebeje (The Royal Palm)
and
Suzanne Alero

Appendix 1 Points of Memorandum to King Philip & His Reply to Dom Domingos[1]

1. **Request for a Reply to letter from Warri.**
   The King apparently had not seen the letter, so he ordered that a reply be sent in general terms.

2. **Request that a Prelate, clergy and regular clergy be sent to Warri.**
   The King approved his Council's suggestion that a good educated priest be sent with two other clergymen. They were too provided with money for the journey and with the necessary ecclesiastical furnishing from the Royal Chapel. The King's Chaplain-in-Chief was to select the priests, making sure they were "tried Christians' but the final approval of his choice was to rest with the King. The King approved the Chaplain's choice in May 1609.

3. **A Request that weapons should be supplied to Warri and arms given to the Prince.**
   The Governor of São Tomé was told to correspond on this matter, with the King of Warri and supply him with whatever they should agreed upon. Dom

1   Culled from: *Dom Domingos in Portugal: The Story of Domingos*--A.F.C. Ryder (1959), In *The Warri Crisis and The Solution*--Committee of Concerned Itsekiris, 1998.

Domingos was to be given a complete suit of steel armor and weapons.

4. **The attention of the King was drawn to the black peppers and other condiments to be found in the Kingdom of Warri.**
    No decision was to be taken until information had been gathered from those who had been there. The Council was to see that they were carefully questioned about the possibilities of this trade.

5. **Request for the conferment of some order. The Prince was to be given robes of the Order of Christ for himself, his father and one brother.**
    In March 1609, the Mesa da Consciencis e Ordens, granted the Orders without the usual rigorous inquiry de genere, considering the "quality" of the candidates! In December 1609, they were dispensed from observation of the customary year and day's novitiate.

6. **Request for exemption from duties on certain things being sent to Warri because they were for the use of churches.**
    This was granted.

7. **Request for more maintenance money until his allowance was paid.**
    He was to be given 500 cruzados on his return from Santiago de Compostela.

8. **Request that his servants be made knight's hidalgos of the Royal Household.**
    Granted for four of them.

9. **Request that an order be conferred on António Martins d'Abreu.**
    Not granted.

10. **A Request that Manoel d'Almeida, his Personal Chaplain, be made a royal chaplain and given a benefice in Madeira.**
    Granted if d'Almeida was adjudged suitable by the Bishop of Madeira.

11. **Request for a passage to Warri in a Royal Ship and for assistance in any Portuguese port in case of shipwreck.**
    He was to sail with ten (10) servants on any ship bound for São Tomé and given all necessary assistance.

Appendix 2 Part of Olu Oyenakpagha's (António Domingos's) letter to Pope Clement X in 1652.[2]

Letter to His Holiness,

The Pope .

Oery City of San Agostinho

20th November 1652

I have been informed of the fervent zeal that burns in the breast of your Holiness to spread the Holy Faith in these parts which, because they have not been watered by the blood of Jesus Christ or any Apostle or Saint, are deprived of the light of the Faith. Also I have heard that to remedy this, your Holiness dispatched a mission of Fathers called Capuchins to the Kingdom of Benin, a people neighboring mine, who rejected the favor offered them and expelled the Fathers from their Kingdom; nor did they tell the Fathers anything about me and my Kingdom. I truly believe, Holy Father,

---

2   A.F.C. Ryder: "Missionary Activity in the Kingdom of Warri in the Early 19th Century." *Journal of Historical Society of Nigeria* Vol. 11, No. 1: 1960. Source: *Benin & Warri*, J.O.S. Ayomike. Mayomi Publishers, Warri, 1993. The Original of this Letter is in Portuguese.

that your Holiness intended these Priests to come to me judging by their information that the King of Benin was a Christian who desired Ministers of the Gospel. I am that King and my Kingdom is on the same coast adjoining Benin and distinguished from it only by the fact that mine is called Oery. As a faithful Christian, I kneel and kiss the feet of your Holiness, and like other Christian Kings, I offer to your Holiness the obedience of myself and my Kingdom and not to your Holiness alone but to all who shall afterwards be elected canonically to that dignity…

I beseech your Holiness to send me some relics for myself and my Kingdom. I am writing to my cousin King John of Portugal asking him to help me by assisting the fathers with their passage and the necessary provisions. I believe he will do this; for the Portuguese have often done me favors; also because they introduced the faith into my Kingdom and my forbearer King Dom Domingos married a Portuguese lady, I hold them in great brotherly affection.

Appendix 3 Inscription on the Headstone of Nuno de Santa Maria.

(Translation)[3]

Here lies that famous Nuno, the Constable, founder of the House of Braganza, excellent General, blessed Monk who during his life on earth so ardently desired the Kingdom of Heaven, that after his death, he merited the eternal company of the Saints.

His worldly honors were countless, but he turned his back on them. He was a great Prince, but he made himself a humble monk.

He founded, built, and endowed this church in which his body rests.

---

3   Source: Wikipedia Contributors: *History of Portugal: Nuno Alvares Pereira,* Wikipedia The Free Encyclopedia. http://enwikipedia.org (accessed April 3, 2009)

References

1. Ayomike, J.O.S. *Benin and Warri. Meeting Points in History.* Warri, Nigeria: Mayomi Publishers. 1993.
2. Ikime, Obaro. *The Merchant Prince of the Niger Delta.* London: Heineman Educational. 1967.
3. Lloyd, P.C. "The Portuguese in Warri." *The Committee of Concerned Itsekiris.* Lagos, Nigeria 1998. 28-33.
4. Lloyd, Christopher. "Part 11, Medieval Misery." *The World: A Pocket History.* London: *Independent.* 2009.
5. Riley-Smith, Jonathan, Ed. *Oxford Illustrated History of the Crusades.* Oxford: Oxford University Press. 1995.
6. Ryder, A.F.C. "The Story of Dom Domingoes." *Odu* No. 4. Ibadan, Nigeria. 1959. 34-40.